How Jesus Built His Church
A Survey of Church History

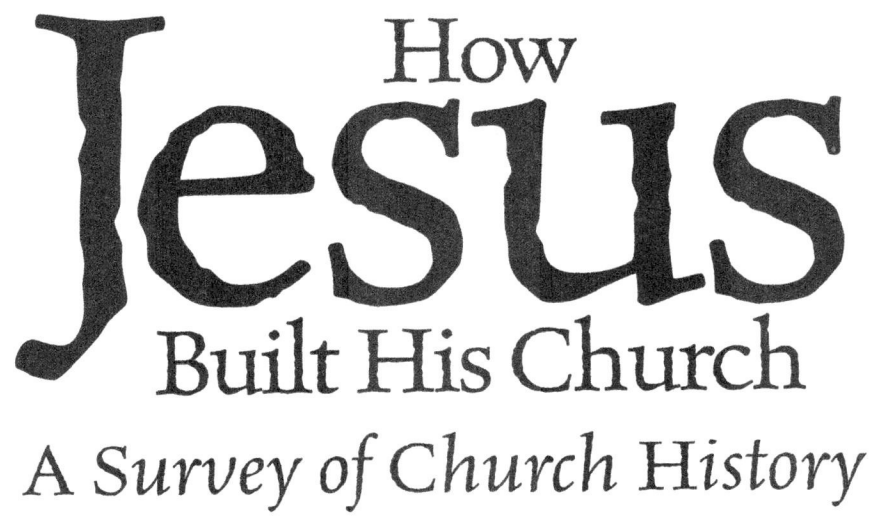

How Jesus Built His Church
A Survey of Church History

STUDENT WORKBOOK

By Joshua Schwisow

Copyright © 2023 by Generations

All rights reserved.
Printed in the United States of America

1st Printing, 2023.

ISBN: 978-1-954745-46-9

Scripture taken from the New King James Version®. Copyright © 1982 by Thomas Nelson. Used by permission. All rights reserved.

Cover Design: Justin Turley
Interior Layout Design: Sarah Lee Bryant and Kyle Shepherd

Published by:
Generations
19039 Plaza Drive Ste 210
Parker, Colorado 80134
www.generations.org

For more information on this and
other titles from Generations,
visit www.generations.org or call 888-389-9080.

Contents

COURSE INTRODUCTION IX

COURSE SCHEDULE XV

WORKSHEETS

Chapter 1: In the Fullness of Time 2

Chapter 2: The Church Faces Opposition 5

Chapter 3: Writings from the Early Church 8

Chapter 4: Christian Worship and Doctrinal Development 11

Chapter 5: Leaders of the Early Church 14

Chapter 6: More Leaders of the Early Church 17

Unit 1 Exam: The Early Church 20

Unit 1 Essay: The Early Church 25

Unit 1 Optional Enrichment Projects 26

Chapter 7: Missionary Expansion 27

Chapter 8: Christian Monasticism 30

Chapter 9: The Rise of Islam 33

Chapter 10: The Development of the Papacy 36

Chapter 11: Schism in the Church 39

Unit 2 Exam: The Early Middle Ages 42

Unit 2 Essay: The Early Middle Ages 47

Unit 2 Optional Enrichment Projects 48

Chapter 12: Universities and Scholasticism 49

Chapter 13: Monasticism in the Middle Ages 52

Chapter 14: The Papal Schism and the Conciliar Movement 55

Chapter 15: Reform Efforts in the Middle Ages. .58

Unit 3 Exam: The Late Middle Ages 61

Unit 3 Essay: The Late Middle Ages. 66

Unit 3 Optional Enrichment Projects 67

Chapter 16: The Dawn of the Reformation 68

Chapter 17: The Reformation in Germany. 70

Chapter 18: The Swiss Reformation in Zurich 73

Chapter 19: The Anabaptist Movement 76

Chapter 20: The Reformation in Geneva. 79

Chapter 21: William Tyndale and the English Bible. 82

Chapter 22: The Reformation in England 85

Chapter 23: The Reformation in Scotland 88

Chapter 24: The Catholic Counter-Reformation. 91

Unit 4 Exam: The Reformation 94

Unit 4 Essay: The Reformation. 99

Unit 4 Optional Enrichment Projects 100

Chapter 25: Puritans, Separatists, and Covenanters 102

Chapter 26: Pietists, Arminians, and Baptists 105

Chapter 27: Christianity in Colonial America 108

Chapter 28: The Great Awakening. 111

Chapter 29: Apostasy and Doctrinal Decline in the Church 113

Unit 5 Exam: The Post-Reformation Period 115

Unit 5 Essay: The Post-Reformation Period 120

Unit 5 Optional Enrichment Projects 121

Chapter 30: The Modern Missionary Movement 123

Chapter 31: Revivals and Cults in the 19th Century. 126

Chapter 32: Fundamentalists and Liberals. 129

Chapter 33: Persecutions in Eastern Europe. 132

Chapter 34: Christians in World War II. 135

Chapter 35: Persecutions in China and Korea 138

Chapter 36: Christian Leaders and Movements of the 20th Century 140

Unit 6 Exam: The Age of Missions and the Modern Period. 143

Unit 6 Essay: The Age of Missions and the Modern Period 148

Unit 6 Optional Enrichment Projects 149

ANSWER KEY **151**

Course Introduction

OVERVIEW

NOTE: It is recommended that the teacher/parent read this Course Introduction, then communicate the specifics to the student for them to understand the expectations of this *How Jesus Built His Church* course.

This course provides a survey of church history worldwide. It spans the period from Christ's birth to the modern day. Successful completion of this course provides the student 1 credit in World History/Church History for a 7th grade reading level. This course is also suitable for other grades including 8th and 9th grade.

This workbook is written for the student who can work mostly independently, yet is still accountable to their teacher/parent. The teacher/parent should determine how much the student could/should do on their own, then the teacher/parent can assist with what the student needs additional help with. It may be that the teacher/parent needs to sit with the student and do all the reading and daily assignments together. It may be that the teacher/parent only needs to check assignments daily, weekly, or monthly to ensure that they are completed and graded. Regardless of the level of parental availability and involvement, we encourage the teacher/parent to engage with their student throughout the school day on this and other subjects being taught or assigned.

I. COMPLETING CHAPTER ASSIGNMENTS

The student should complete the chapter assignments after reading the assigned first or second half of each chapter. In order to prepare for these chapter assignments. As the student reads, they should underline or highlight key dates, events, locations, persons, or list them in a separate notebook. Upon completion of the reading, the student should complete the related chapter assignments open-book.

II. COMPLETING UNIT EXAMS

The student should review their completed open-book chapter assignments in the days before completing the six end-of-unit exams. These unit exams are to be completed "closed book." Students must use their memory to accurately answer the questions.

III. COURSE OBJECTIVES

This course has been prepared by authors and editors who are committed to the glory of God and to the preeminence of the Lord Jesus Christ in all things. Therefore, the essential objectives for the student must be:

1. That all who study this course would give God the glory for His sovereignty, His power, His goodness, His judgments, and His mercy.

2. That the student would recognize that Jesus Christ is indeed King of kings and Lord of lords.

3. That the student would see how God works through the lives of individual disciples of the Lord Jesus Christ, who by God's grace, are used for the furtherance of the kingdom of Jesus Christ.

4. That the student would find relevance in these historical studies for himself or herself; that these studies would render meaning and purpose to history and to the lives we live.

5. That the student would better understand the times in which he/she lives, given an understanding of what has gone before.

6. That the student would gain an optimism about the kingdom of God worldwide, even as the kingdoms of men rise and fall.

7. That the student would have a mind and an eye for the important events in history, as defined by a biblical world and life view.

8. That the student would know Scripture better and see its amazing relevance to history and life, especially as the many Scripture references are read through the duration of this course.

IV. COURSE SCHEDULE

The course schedule included in this workbook is a suggestion. The teacher/parent and student may adapt the schedule to suit their needs. The course schedule is based on a 36-week school year divided into two semesters, covering 36 chapters of reading.

In most cases, 3 days per week are required to complete the assignment. The other 2 days of the week can be used to catch up if necessary. On weeks where unit exams and unit essays are assigned, there will be 5 days of coursework assigned.

V. OPTIONAL ENRICHMENT PROJECTS

Each unit ends with a series of recommended optional enrichment projects (OEPs). These enrichment projects provide an opportunity for the student to reinforce what they have learned by doing something active with their knowledge. They are also meant to stretch the student in their ability and productivity with new and perhaps challenging activities that are based on different learning styles.

OEPs are not to be graded. Their outcome may be used as "extra credit" for the mid- and end-of-year grades, if the parent/teacher decides to include them.

Note, often OEPs take additional time, beyond what is noted on the lesson schedule. It is recommended that the parent/teacher provide additional flexibility on completion of the OEPs.

VI. GRADING CHAPTER ASSIGNMENTS

The teacher/parent should determine how to grade the assignments and discuss their decision with the student. Assignments can be ungraded, graded on a pass/fail system, or using letter grades based on percentages. We offer these suggested guidelines for the parent/teacher to grade assignments using the percentage/letter method.

For example, if 12 out of 15 chapter assignment questions were answered correctly, then the percentage grade for that chapter will be 80%.

12 divided by 15 = 12/15 = 80%

VII. GRADING UNIT EXAMS

The teacher/parent should grade the quarterly exams like the previously mentioned assignments by dividing the number of correctly answered questions by the total number of questions. Once the percentage is known, a letter grade can be assigned as noted in the section below on Grade Values.

VIII. GRADE VALUES

The following may be used for grade values when grading chapter assignments, exams, or projects by percentages:

90 to 100 percent = A
80-89 percent = B
70 to 79 percent = C
60 to 69 percent = D
0 to 59 percent = F

IX. PRAYER POINTS

Each chapter assignment ends with a section on prayer. Once the student reaches the end of the chapter assignments, they should take time to pray in light of the prayer suggestions provided. This is one of the ways the student applies what they learn about Christ's church. If we are to seek the kingdom of Jesus first (Matt. 6:33), prayer is one of the ways that we do this ("*your kingdom come, your will be done on earth as it is heaven*"). These prayer suggestions are also a great opportunity to involve the whole family in praying for the nations during regular prayer time at shared meals or family devotions.

X. OTHER SUGGESTED COURSE SUPPLIES

It is helpful in this course for the student to have these basic school supplies:

1. A package of lined index cards, either white or in various colors; these will be used for group discussion prompts and presentation activities for some of the Optional Enrichment Projects (OEPs). A ziplock bag or other container for the cards will keep them from getting lost.

2. A 3-ring notebook with lined paper and some plain white unlined paper, in which they can learn to take notes as they read through the chapters. Alternatively, a spiral notebook with pockets for added blank white pages will suffice.

3. Construction paper, crayon/color markers/color pencils, glue, regular (black) pencils, poster boards, 12" stick ruler, and unlined white paper for OEPs.

4. A Bible in the family's preferred translation.

XI. TEACHING METHOD

In order for this course to have maximum effect, the teacher/parent should consider the importance of life application and enrichment, tying in other aspects of learning (besides the textbook and this workbook). These might include:

- Discuss what the student is learning in informal contexts such as dinner time or car rides.

- Listen to the "World View in 5 Minutes" to stay updated on what God has done in His Story over the last 24-hours. This is an online daily radio broadcast, which can be found at https://theworldview.com/, or as the lead-in to Kevin Swanson's online daily radio broadcasts found at https://www.generations.org/

radio. (Remember, the news is only the last 24 hours of history. It is important to update the student on current events, from a biblical worldview perspective.)

- Use three-dimensional experiences like field trips and family vacations to historical sites as a means of enriching these historical studies. For overseas experiences virtually, utilize your local library or the internet to watch history or travel videos. We want to impress on our children the significance of places and times where God worked and brought about amazing developments in world history.

XII. YOUR STUDENT'S SAFE AND APPROPRIATE USE OF THE INTERNET FOR THIS WORKBOOK

Some of the projects in this workbook suggest that your student use the internet, which can be an educational tool for learning. In our culture now and into the future, nearly all teens and adults will need to use it for their daily life, including for school, work, or leisure activities. For a young person to successfully navigate this technology, parents need to help them learn how to use it safely and appropriately. Parents need to set boundaries to avoid overuse and addiction. Please consider allowing your student to do this type of research with your guidance and supervision. If you do not have parental controls on the device they will use, it is suggested you do the research with them for close monitoring.

NOTE: If the teacher/parent determines using the internet is not something their student should do as part of this workbook, then the teacher/parent should encourage their student to use print resources available in a family library or a public library.

For Christ's Kingdom,
Joshua Schwisow
The Generations Curriculum Team
January AD 2023

Course Schedule

Suggested Lesson Schedule

Day	Assignment	Due Date	✓	Grade
FIRST SEMESTER—FIRST QUARTER				
WEEK 1				
1	Read Introduction	7/15/24	✓	
2	Begin Reading Chapter 1	7/16/24	✓	
3	Finish Reading Chapter 1	7/17/24	✓	
4	Flex Day	7/18/24	✓	
5	Complete Chapter 1 Assignments	7/19/24	✓	88%
WEEK 2				
1	Begin Reading Chapter 2	7/22/24	✓	
2	Flex Day			
3	Finish Reading Chapter 2	7/24/24	✓	
4	Flex Day			
5	Complete Chapter 2 Assignments	7/30/24	✓	88%
WEEK 3				
1	Begin Reading Chapter 3	8/2/24	✓	
2	Flex Day			
3	Finish Reading Chapter 3	8/5/24	✓	
4	Flex Day			
5	Complete Chapter 3 Assignments	8/8/24	✓	96%

COURSE SCHEDULE XVII

Day	Assignment	Due Date	✓	Grade
WEEK 4				
1	Begin Reading Chapter 4	8/20/24	✓	
2	Flex Day			
3	Finish Reading Chapter 4	8/20/24	✓	
4	Flex Day			
5	Complete Chapter 4 Assignments	8/23/24		
WEEK 5				
1	Begin Reading Chapter 5			
2	Flex Day			
3	Finish Reading Chapter 5			
4	Flex Day			
5	Complete Chapter 5 Assignments			
WEEK 6				
1	Begin Reading Chapter 6			
2	Finish Reading Chapter 6			
3	Complete Chapter 6 Assignments			
4	Complete Unit 1 Exam			
5	Complete Chapter 1 Essay and Select Unit 1 OEP			
WEEK 7				
1	Begin Reading Chapter 7			
2	Flex Day			
3	Finish Reading Chapter 7			

Day	Assignment	Due Date	✓	Grade
4	Flex Day			
5	Complete Chapter 7 Assignments			

WEEK 8

Day	Assignment	Due Date	✓	Grade
1	Begin Reading Chapter 8			
2	Flex Day			
3	Finish Reading Chapter 8			
4	Flex Day			
5	Complete Chapter 8 Assignments			

WEEK 9

Day	Assignment	Due Date	✓	Grade
1	Begin Reading Chapter 9			
2	Flex Day			
3	Finish Reading Chapter 9			
4	Flex Day			
5	Complete Chapter 9 Assignments			

FIRST SEMESTER—SECOND QUARTER

WEEK 10

Day	Assignment	Due Date	✓	Grade
1	Begin Reading Chapter 10			
2	Flex Day			
3	Finish Reading Chapter 10			
4	Flex Day			
5	Complete Chapter 10 Assignments			

COURSE SCHEDULE XIX

Day	Assignment	Due Date	✓	Grade
WEEK 11				
1	Begin Reading Chapter 11			
2	Finish Reading Chapter 11			
3	Complete Chapter 11 Assignments			
4	Complete Unit 2 Exam			
5	Complete Unit 2 Essay and Select Unit 2 OEP			
WEEK 12				
1	Begin Reading Chapter 12			
2	Flex Day			
3	Finish Reading Chapter 12			
4	Flex Day			
5	Complete Chapter 12 Assignments			
WEEK 13				
1	Begin Reading Chapter 13			
2	Flex Day			
3	Finish Reading Chapter 13			
4	Flex Day			
5	Complete Chapter 13 Assignments			
WEEK 14				
1	Begin Reading Chapter 14			
2	Flex Day			
3	Finish Reading Chapter 14			

Day	Assignment	Due Date	✓	Grade
4	Flex Day			
5	Complete Chapter 14 Assignments			

WEEK 15

Day	Assignment	Due Date	✓	Grade
1	Begin Reading Chapter 15			
2	Finish Reading Chapter 15			
3	Complete Chapter 15 Assignments			
4	Complete Unit 3 Exam			
5	Complete Unit 3 Essay and Select Unit 3 OEP			

WEEK 16

Day	Assignment	Due Date	✓	Grade
1	Begin Reading Chapter 16			
2	Flex Day			
3	Finish Reading Chapter 16			
4	Flex Day			
5	Complete Chapter 16 Assignments			

WEEK 17

Day	Assignment	Due Date	✓	Grade
1	Begin Reading Chapter 17			
2	Flex Day			
3	Finish Reading Chapter 17			
4	Flex Day			
5	Complete Chapter 17 Assignments			

WEEK 18

Day	Assignment	Due Date	✓	Grade
1	Begin Reading Chapter 18			

Day	Assignment	Due Date	✓	Grade
2	Flex Day			
3	Finish Reading Chapter 18			
4	Flex Day			
5	Complete Chapter 18 Assignments			
MIDTERM GRADE				

SECOND SEMESTER—THIRD QUARTER

WEEK 19

Day	Assignment	Due Date	✓	Grade
1	Begin Reading Chapter 19			
2	Flex Day			
3	Finish Reading Chapter 19			
4	Flex Day			
5	Complete Chapter 19 Assignments			

WEEK 20

Day	Assignment	Due Date	✓	Grade
1	Begin Reading Chapter 20			
2	Flex Day			
3	Finish Reading Chapter 20			
4	Flex Day			
5	Complete Chapter 20 Assignments			

WEEK 21

Day	Assignment	Due Date	✓	Grade
1	Begin Reading Chapter 21			
2	Flex Day			
3	Finish Reading Chapter 21			

Day	Assignment	Due Date	✓	Grade
4	Flex Day			
5	Complete Chapter 21 Assignments			
WEEK 22				
1	Begin Reading Chapter 22			
2	Flex Day			
3	Finish Reading Chapter 22			
4	Flex Day			
5	Complete Chapter 22 Assignments			
WEEK 23				
1	Begin Reading Chapter 23			
2	Flex Day			
3	Finish Reading Chapter 23			
4	Flex Day			
5	Complete Chapter 23 Assignments			
WEEK 24				
1	Begin Reading Chapter 24			
2	Finish Reading Chapter 24			
3	Complete Chapter 24 Assignments			
4	Complete Unit 4 Exam			
5	Complete Unit 4 Essay and Select Unit 4 OEP			
WEEK 25				
1	Begin Reading Chapter 25			
2	Flex Day			

COURSE SCHEDULE XXIII

Day	Assignment	Due Date	✓	Grade
3	Finish Reading Chapter 25			
4	Flex Day			
5	Complete Chapter 25 Assignments			

WEEK 26

Day	Assignment	Due Date	✓	Grade
1	Begin Reading Chapter 26			
2	Flex Day			
3	Finish Reading Chapter 26			
4	Flex Day			
5	Complete Chapter 26 Assignments			

WEEK 27

Day	Assignment	Due Date	✓	Grade
1	Begin Reading Chapter 27			
2	Flex Day			
3	Finish Reading Chapter 27			
4	Flex Day			
5	Complete Chapter 27 Assignments			

SECOND SEMESTER—FOURTH QUARTER

WEEK 28

Day	Assignment	Due Date	✓	Grade
1	Begin Reading Chapter 28			
2	Flex Day			
3	Finish Reading Chapter 28			
4	Flex Day			
5	Complete Chapter 28 Assignments			

Day	Assignment	Due Date	✓	Grade
WEEK 29				
1	Begin Reading Chapter 29			
2	Finish Reading Chapter 28			
3	Complete Chapter 29 Assignments			
4	Complete Unit 5 Exam			
5	Complete Unit 5 Essay and Select Unit 5 OEP			
WEEK 30				
1	Begin Reading Chapter 30			
2	Flex Day			
3	Finish Reading Chapter 30			
4	Flex Day			
5	Complete Chapter 30 Assignments			
WEEK 31				
1	Begin Reading Chapter 31			
2	Flex Day			
3	Finish Reading Chapter 31			
4	Flex Day			
5	Complete Chapter 31 Assignments			
WEEK 32				
1	Begin Reading Chapter 32			
2	Flex Day			
3	Finish Reading Chapter 32			
4	Flex Day			

Day	Assignment	Due Date	✓	Grade
5	Complete Chapter 32 Assignments			

WEEK 33

Day	Assignment	Due Date	✓	Grade
1	Begin Reading Chapter 33			
2	Flex Day			
3	Finish Reading Chapter 33			
4	Flex Day			
5	Complete Chapter 33 Assignments			

WEEK 34

Day	Assignment	Due Date	✓	Grade
1	Begin Reading Chapter 34			
2	Flex Day			
3	Finish Reading Chapter 34			
4	Flex Day			
5	Complete Chapter 34 Assignments			

WEEK 35

Day	Assignment	Due Date	✓	Grade
1	Begin Reading Chapter 35			
2	Flex Day			
3	Finish Reading Chapter 35			
4	Flex Day			
5	Complete Chapter 35 Assignments			

WEEK 36

Day	Assignment	Due Date	✓	Grade
1	Begin Reading Chapter 36			
2	Finish Reading Chapter 36			

Day	Assignment	Due Date	✓	Grade
3	Complete Chapter 36 Assignments			
4	Complete Unit 6 Exam			
5	Complete Unit 6 Essay and Select Unit 6 OEP			
FINAL GRADE				

Worksheets

1. In the Fullness of Time

TIMELINE AND LOCATION REVIEW

1. The Emperor Nero reigned over from the Roman Empire from AD __54__ to AD __68__.

2. A likely date for Paul's execution is AD __67__.

3. John was exiled to the isle of __Patmos__.

4. The coming of the Holy Spirit on the Day of Pentecost occurred in the city of __Jerusalem__.

5. Our Lord Jesus promised that His disciples would be witnesses to the four regions mentioned in Acts 1 including ~~everywhere~~ __Judea__, __Jerusalem__, __Samaria__, and to the __ends__ of the earth.

SHORT ANSWER

6. What does BC stand for?
   Before Christ

7. What does AD stand for?
   Anno Domini

8. Which of the Gospel writers records the angel's announcement of Christ's birth to the shepherds?
   Luke

9. What do we call the monumental mission Jesus gave to His disciples?
   The Great Commission

10. What happened on the Day of Pentecost?

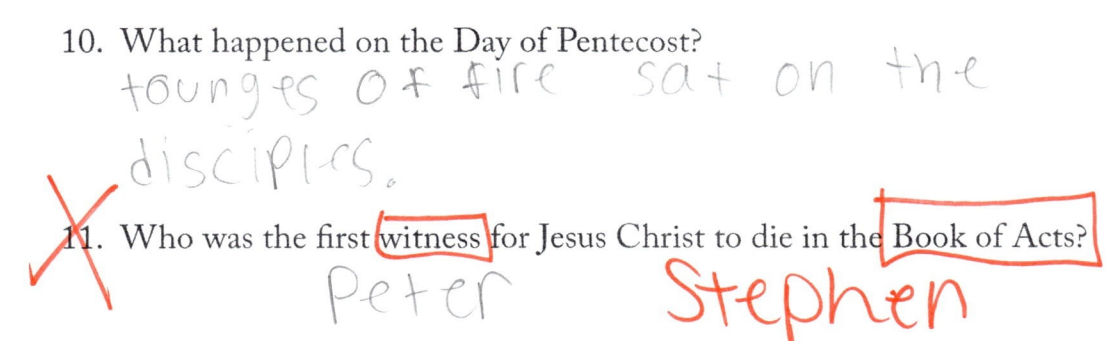

    tounges of fire sat on the disciples.

11. Who was the first witness for Jesus Christ to die in the Book of Acts?

    Peter Stephen

12. Approximately how many miles did Paul cover in his second missionary journey?

    2,800 miles

13. According to historical records, during whose reign was Paul executed?

    emperor Nero

14. Which books of the New Testament did the Apostle John write?

    Romans, 1,2 corinthians, Galatians, Ephesians, Philipians, colossians, 1,2 thessalonians, 1,2 timothy, titus, Philemon,

15. In what city was Paul in when he observed the statue to the "unknown God"?

    Mars Hill, in Athens

HEARING FROM GOD'S WORD

16. Read Ephesians 2:19-20. What is described as the foundation of the church? Who is the cornerstone of the church?

    The foundation is the apostles and prophets. The cornerstone is Jesus.

17. Read Acts 9:31. How does Luke describe the health of the growing church in this verse? *The church had peace and became stronger.*

PRAYER

Now, take time to pray a prayer of thanksgiving, praise, and petition to our great God.

- Praise God for His wisdom and sovereignty in sending His Son, the Lord Jesus Christ, in the fullness of time to save us from our sins. Acknowledge God to be all-wise, all-powerful, and merciful in His plan and accomplishment of redemption.

- Ask the Lord to bless your local church with the work of the Holy Spirit described in Acts 9:31. Pray that your church would be multiplied. Pray that the people of your church would walk in the fear of God, and that they would experience the comfort of the Holy Spirit, and that they would experience peace in the Lord and with one another.

2. The Church Faces Opposition

−2

TIMELINE AND LOCATION REVIEW

1. A fire broke out in Rome in AD __64__ during Nero's reign.

2. The Emperor Domitian reigned from AD __81__ to AD __96__.

3. A severe persecution occurred in the south of France (Gaul) in AD __177__.

4. The Battle of Milvian Bridge occurred in AD __312__.

5. ~~The persecution in France (Gaul) occurred during the reign of Emperor __Domitian__.~~ Marcus Aurelius
   Pg 29

SHORT ANSWER

6. Why were Christians called "atheists" by some in the Roman Empire?
   Because they didn't believe in false Roman gods.

7. Which Roman historian recorded how Nero blamed the Christians for the fire in Rome?
   The Roman named Tacitus.

8. Which Church historian records that Peter and Paul were executed in Rome?
   Eusebius records this.

9. Define the terms *religio licita* and *religio illicita*.
   Lawful religion   Unlawful religion

10. During whose reign did the "Great Persecution" occur?
    During the reign of Nero.
    Diocletian   Pg 29-30

11. Which of Christ's disciples personally taught Polycarp?
    John taught Polycarp.

12. What was the name of the young woman who was martyred in Lyons around AD 177? Her name was Blandina

13. Which Roman emperor made Sunday a day of rest and exempted churches from taxation? Constantine

14. In what early church document do we find the account of Polycarp?
    The Martyrdom of Polycarp.

15. What does the word "martyr" mean?
    It means "witness"

HEARING FROM GOD'S WORD

16. Read 1 Peter 1:6-7. What are the effects of trials in the life of believers?
    It will bring you praise and honor and glory.

17. Read Acts 14:21-22. What is described here as an absolute necessity?

We must go through tribulation.

PRAYER

Now, take time to pray a prayer of thanksgiving and praise to the Lord Almighty. Also, ask the Lord to strengthen you, and your fellow Christians for trials you will meet.

- Praise God for the power of the Holy Spirit which is evident in the boldness, faith, and love of Christian martyrs past and present.

- Praise God for sustaining the church through many persecutions and growing it despite the fury and malice of Satan.

- Ask the Lord to grow you in boldness as a witness for Jesus Christ. Ask God to strengthen your family and your local church to increasingly be faithful witnesses to the Lord, not fearing slander, reproach, or persecution.

3. Writings from the Early Church

TIMELINE MATCHING

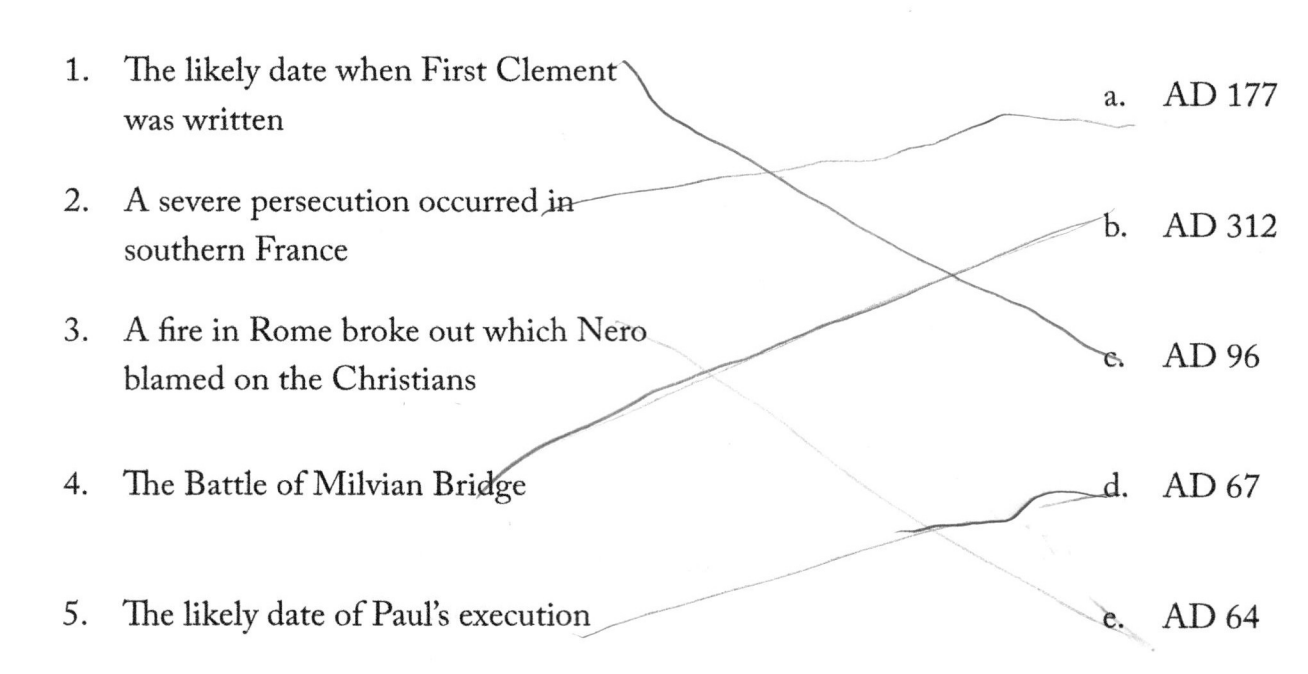

1. The likely date when First Clement was written
2. A severe persecution occurred in southern France
3. A fire in Rome broke out which Nero blamed on the Christians
4. The Battle of Milvian Bridge
5. The likely date of Paul's execution

a. AD 177
b. AD 312
c. AD 96
d. AD 67
e. AD 64

SHORT ANSWER

6. What is the earliest collection of documents written by Christians after the New Testament called? Shepard of Hermas, the Epistles of Barnabas, and the Didache.

½

7. To what church was *First Clement* written?
to the Church of Corinth.

8. How many letters did Ignatius of Antioch write?
Ingnatius wrote seven letters.

HOW JESUS BUILT HIS CHURCH WORKBOOK 9

9. ~~What three offices of church government does Ignatius present in his letter?~~ Bishop, elders, deacons
   no. 1, the unity of the church.
   no. 2, opposing false teachers
   no. 3, his impending martyrdom

10. Which early church manual of doctrine and practice provides instruction on baptism? The Didache has instruction on baptism.

11. Who wrote the *Letter to Diognetus*?
    We do not know.

12. What is the name of the early church manual in Syriac mentioned in this chapter?
    Didascalia Apostolorum

13. Who wrote the first extensive summary of Church History?
    Eusebius

HEARING FROM GOD'S WORD

14. Read Philippians 1:1-2. What two offices does Paul mention in his address to the church in Philippi? He mentions overseers and deacons.

15. Read 1 Corinthians 13. Then, review the quotation in the textbook from *First Clement* where Clement speaks on the nature of love. List some of the similar descriptions of love you see in both 1 Corinthians 13 and *First Clement*.

    love is patient   Love does not boast

    Love is not proud

PRAYER

Now, take time to call upon the name of the Lord, giving thanks to Him, and asking Him to grant spiritual blessings to you and to the church of Jesus Christ.

- Thank the Lord first for His Spirit-inspired and infallible Word, the written Word of God. Praise the Lord for the perfection of His Word, and the many blessings that flow from the meditation and application of that Word.

- Thank the Lord for faithful teachers of the early church who wrote edifying documents for the instruction of Christ's people.

- Pray that God would grow you, your family, and your local church in Christian love, which is the greatest of Christian virtues (1 Cor. 13:13).

4. Christian Worship and Doctrinal Development

PERSON MATCHING

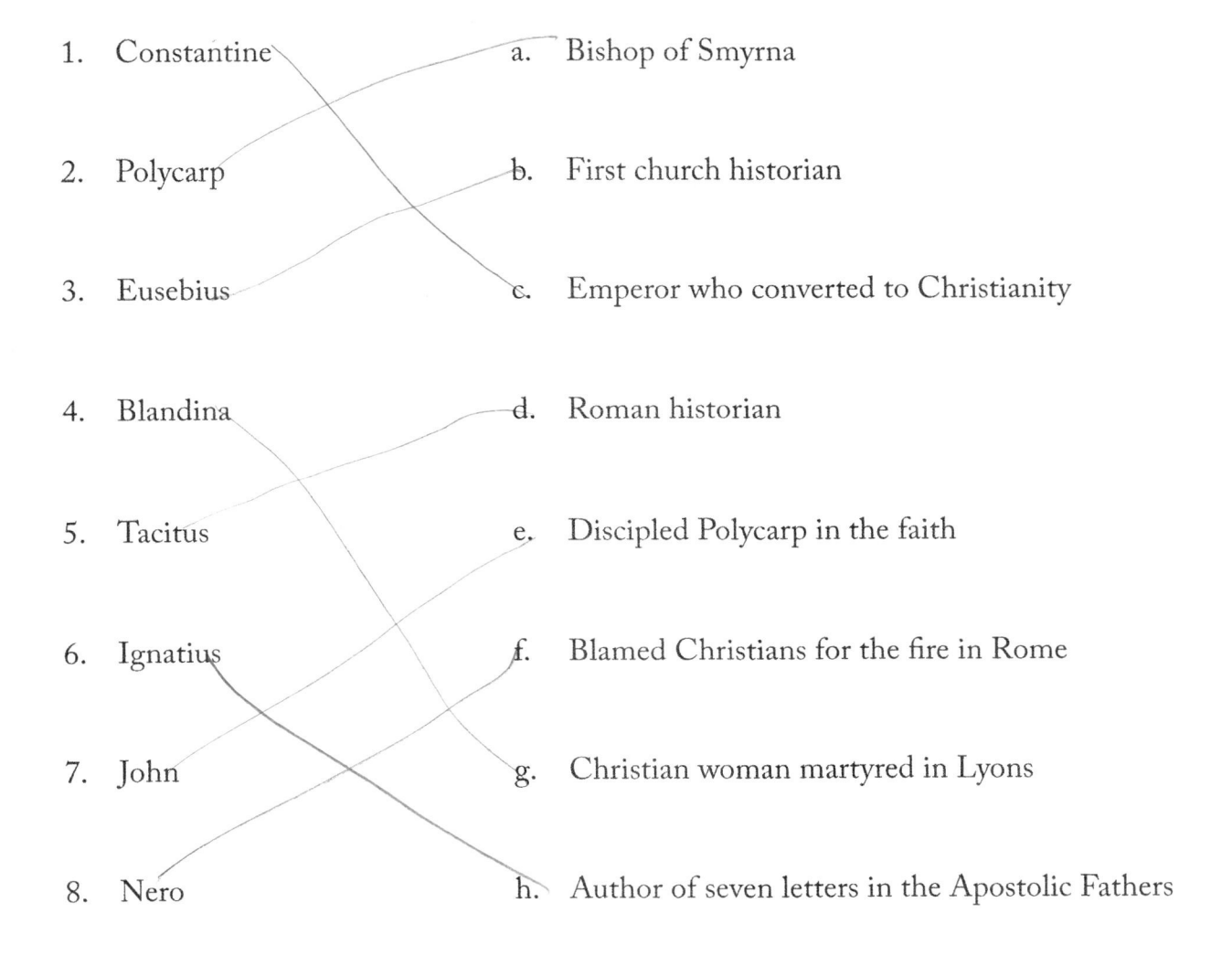

1. Constantine — c. Emperor who converted to Christianity
2. Polycarp — a. Bishop of Smyrna
3. Eusebius — b. First church historian
4. Blandina — g. Christian woman martyred in Lyons
5. Tacitus — d. Roman historian
6. Ignatius — h. Author of seven letters in the Apostolic Fathers
7. John — e. Discipled Polycarp in the faith
8. Nero — f. Blamed Christians for the fire in Rome

SHORT ANSWER

9. On what day of the week did the early church gather for worship?

   Sunday

10. What do we learn about baptism in the early church from Hippolytus?
    That Baptism was an essential rite for disciples.

11. What two early church fathers are cited as examples in support of infant baptism?
    Cyprian and Hippolytus

12. Which church father mentions infant baptism but was against it?
    Tertullian

13. Why did early Christians use the fish as a symbol of early Christianity?
    as a symbol of Jesus feeding the five thousand

14. How did early Christians respond to the practice of abortion in Roman society?
    They saved as many kids as they could

15. What former slave became bishop of Rome?
    Ignatius

16. What church council condemned the teaching of Arius? When did it occur?
    Council of Niceaea at AD 325

17. What church council declared that Jesus Christ was one person with two natures? When did it occur?
    The council of Chalcedon AD 451

18. Which significant early church father wrote against the teachings of Pelagius?
    Augustine of Hippo

HEARING FROM GOD'S WORD

19. Read Acts 2:41-42. What components are described about the worship and fellowship of the early church? *they were baptized, they broke bread, and prayed.*

20. Read 1 Peter 4:1-5. Focus on vs. 4. If Christians are living according to God's will, what does Peter say will be the response of unbelievers to Christians? *They will be surprised you don't join them.*

PRAYER

Now, spend time in prayer coming to the Father of lights, from whom every blessing comes.

- Thank the Lord for faithful pastors and teachers who defended the truth of God's Word against Satan's attacks.

- Thank the Lord for the privilege of participating in the weekly fellowship and worship of Christ's church.

- Ask the Lord to grow you as an edifying member of the body of Christ. Ask the Lord to show you how to use your gifts to contribute to the strengthening of the church body.

- Pray for your local pastors/elders to be faithful in maintaining sound doctrine and that they would be godly examples to Christ's flock.

5. Leaders of the Early Church

TIMELINE AND LOCATION REVIEW

1. Irenaeus was the bishop of the city of _____.

2. Clement of Alexandria died in AD _____.

3. Tertullian joined the Montanists in AD _____.

4. The Second Council of Constantinople declared Origen a heretic in AD _____.

5. Origen was a teacher in the city of _____.

PERSON MATCHING

6. Marcion

7. Septimius Severus

8. Tertullian

9. Origen

10. Clement of Alexandria

11. Augustine

a. as a young man, he was eager to die as a martyr for Christ

b. believed that Christian teaching was consistent with much of Plato's writings

c. Roman emperor who persecuted Christians around AD 202

d. heretic who created his own reduced canon of Scripture

e. wrote against the teachings of Pelagius

f. early church leader who lived in Carthage

SHORT ANSWER

12. Who wrote *Against Heresies*?

13. Who coined the word "Trinity"?

14. How does this chapter describe Origen's approach to interpreting Scripture?

15. What did Tertullian think about pagan philosophy?

16. What are some characteristics of Tertullian's writings?

17. What is a catechumen?

HEARING FROM GOD'S WORD

18. Read Colossians 2:8-10. What warning does Paul give in this passage? How might we apply this warning in the modern-day to teaching we encounter?

19. Read Ephesians 4:14-16. According to this passage, how do we grow in Christian maturity?

PRAYER

Now, take time to pray to Almighty God, who is able to do above all that we ask or think (Eph. 3:20-21).

- Give thanks to the Lord for faithful church shepherds from the past and in the present. Thank the Lord Jesus Christ for equipping His church with those who feed God's people with knowledge and understanding.

- Ask the Lord Jesus to purify the church in your country of false doctrine and ungodly behavior.

- Pray that the Lord would mature you in Christ and ask the Lord to use you to edify and build up others in the church body.

- Ask the Lord to grow you in discernment so that you can approve those things which are excellent (Phil. 1:9-10), and reject those things which are not true.

6. More Leaders of the Early Church

TIMELINE MATCHING

1. The Council of Nicaea — a. 361
2. Julian the Apostate becomes emperor — b. 410
3. Ambrose becomes bishop of Milan — c. 404
4. The Council of Chalcedon — d. 325
5. Augustine is born — e. 354
6. Rome captured and sacked — f. 373
7. Vandals capture Hippo — g. 451
8. Jerome completes his Latin translation of the Bible — h. 430

SHORT ANSWER

9. Who defended the teaching of the Nicene Creed against Arians and served as a bishop in Alexandria for many years?

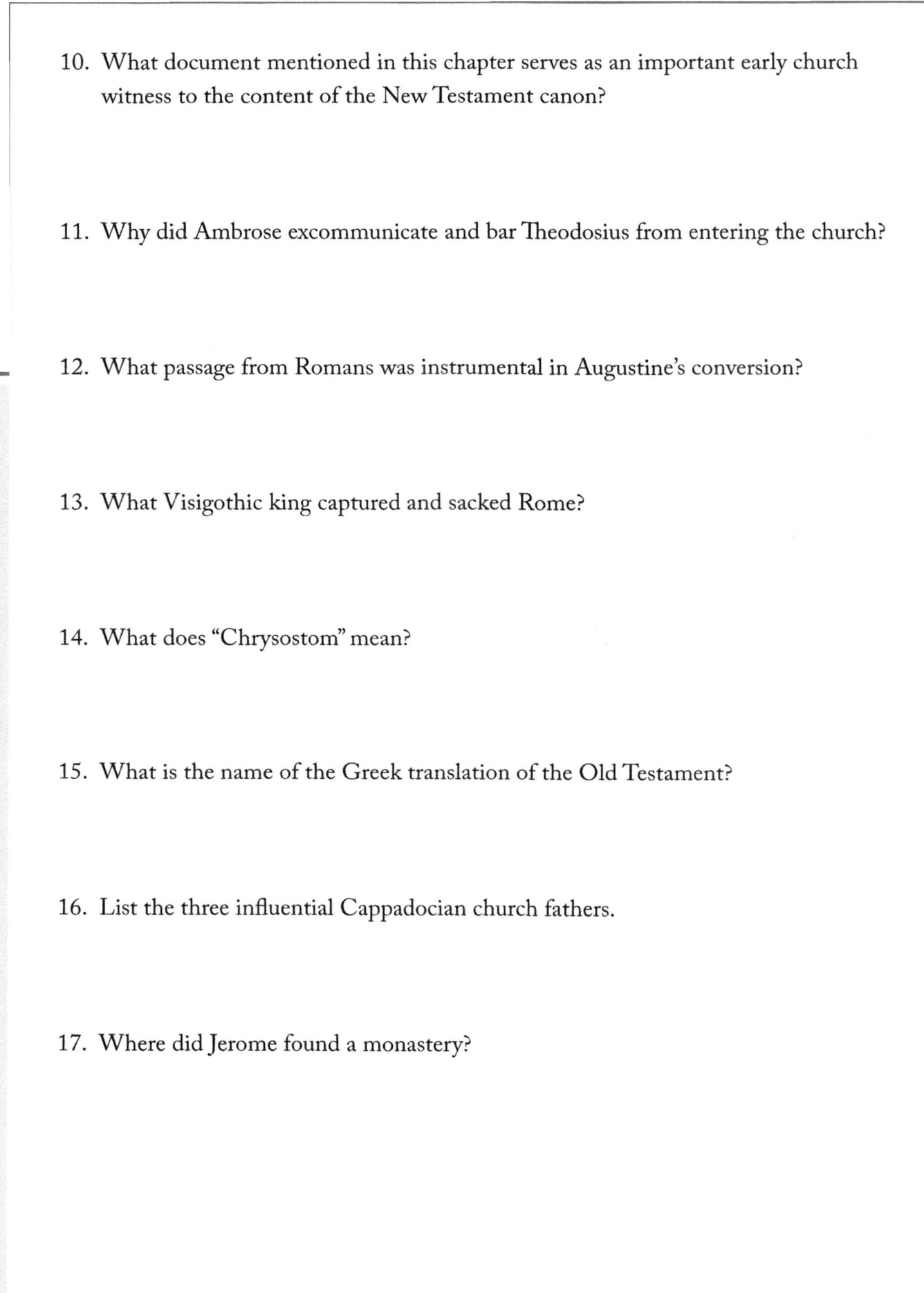

10. What document mentioned in this chapter serves as an important early church witness to the content of the New Testament canon?

11. Why did Ambrose excommunicate and bar Theodosius from entering the church?

12. What passage from Romans was instrumental in Augustine's conversion?

13. What Visigothic king captured and sacked Rome?

14. What does "Chrysostom" mean?

15. What is the name of the Greek translation of the Old Testament?

16. List the three influential Cappadocian church fathers.

17. Where did Jerome found a monastery?

HEARING FROM GOD'S WORD

18. Read 1 Peter 5:1-4. What are some of the characteristics of a faithful elder?

19. Read Ephesians 4:11-12. Why did Jesus Christ give pastors and teachers to the church?

PRAYER

Now, take some time to seek the face of the Lord in prayer.

- Praise God for the work of faithful pastors/shepherds who have been faithful leaders for Christ's people both in the past and in the present.

- Thank the Lord for giving gifts to the body of Christ so that it can grow.

- Ask the Lord to guide you in taking what you have learned in Christian discipleship and using it to minister to others.

- Pray that the Lord would guide the preaching and teaching ministry of your local church so that it would be a ministry that would be faithful, Spirit-filled, and truly edifying.

Unit 1 Exam: The Early Church

Total: 40 Points

TIMELINE MATCHING

1. The Council of Chalcedon   a. 325

2. Vandals capture Hippo   b. 451

3. The Battle of Milvian Bridge   c. 410

4. The Council of Nicaea   d. 96

5. A severe persecution occurs in southern France   e. 553

6. A fire in Rome breaks out which Nero blames on the Christians f. 177

7. Rome captured and sacked   g. 312

8. The likely date when *First Clement* was written   h. 64

9. Augustine is born   i. 430

10. The Second Council of Constantinople declares Origen a heretic j. 354

PERSON MATCHING

11. Constantine

12. Nero

13. Eusebius

14. Ignatius

15. Polycarp

16. Tertullian

17. Origen

18. Augustine

19. Marcion

20. Tacitus

a. Early church leader who lived in Carthage

b. Author of seven letters in the Apostolic Fathers

c. As a young man, he was eager to die as a martyr for Christ

d. Blamed Christians for the fire in Rome

e. Wrote against the teachings of Pelagius

f. Roman emperor who converted to Christianity

g. Heretic who created his own reduced canon of Scripture

h. First church historian

i. Roman historian

j. Bishop of Smyrna

MULTIPLE CHOICE

21. Served as Bishop of Hippo
    A. Tertullian
    B. Origen
    C. Augustine
    D. Irenaeus

22. Gospel writer who records the angels announcing Jesus' birth to the shepherds
    A. Matthew
    B. Mark
    C. Luke
    D. John

23. The first martyr to die in the Book of Acts
    A. James
    B. Stephen
    C. Peter
    D. John

24. The "Great Persecution" occurred during the reign of which emperor?
    A. Diocletian
    B. Domitian
    C. Nero
    D. Decius

25. Martyred in Lyons during the reign of Emperor Marcus Aurelius
    A. Polycarp
    B. Ignatius
    C. Stephen
    D. Blandina

26. Constantine defeated who at the Battle of Milvian Bridge?
    A. Galerius
    B. Maxentius
    C. Licinius
    D. Diocletian

27. Which of these documents is NOT a part of the collection known as the Apostolic Fathers?
    A. Letters of Ignatius
    B. *First Clement*
    C. *The Didache*
    D. *Didascalia Apostolorum*

28. Which of these documents served as an apology, or defense, of the Christian faith?
    A. *The Shepherd of Hermas*
    B. *The Martyrdom of Polycarp*
    C. *The Letter to Diognetus*
    D. *The Didache*

29. Which of these early church fathers mentions the practice of infant baptism but was against it?
    A. Tertullian
    B. Hippolytus
    C. Cyprian
    D. Augustine

30. Ignatius of Antioch advocated for this form of church government
    A. Elders and Deacons
    B. Pope, Bishops, Elders, Deacons
    C. Bishops, Elders, Deacons
    D. Archbishop, Bishop, Elders, Deacons

31. The Council of Chalcedon taught this about Jesus:
    A. Jesus Christ has two personalities with two natures
    B. Jesus Christ is one person with two natures
    C. Jesus Christ is one person with one nature
    D. Jesus Christ has two personalities with one nature

32. Who taught that man is NOT born corrupt in sin?
    A. Pelagius
    B. Augustine
    C. Arius
    D. Nestorius

33. Irenaeus wrote against which heretical group in *Against Heresies*?
    A. Arianism
    B. Sabellianism
    C. Gnosticism
    D. Pelagianism

34. Which early church father believed that pagan philosophy and Christian thought were irreconcilable?
    A. Clement
    B. Origen
    C. Augustine
    D. Tertullian

35. Who coined the term "Trinity"?
    A. Tertullian
    B. Origen
    C. Irenaeus
    D. Augustine

36. What was the name of the bishop who preceded Athanasius in Alexandria?
    A. Arius
    B. Alexander
    C. Ulfilas
    D. Julius

37. Who served as bishop in Milan?
    A. Ambrose
    B. Augustine
    C. Origen
    D. Clement

38. Who wrote *The City of God*?
    A. Ambrose
    B. Origen
    C. Athanasius
    D. Augustine

39. Who created the Bible translation known as the Latin Vulgate?

    A. Augustine
    B. Ambrose
    C. Jerome
    D. Athanasius

40. Who was exiled from Constantinople for his bold preaching?

    A. Jerome
    B. John Chrysostom
    C. Athanasius
    D. Ambrose

Unit 1 Essay: The Early Church

Write an essay of at least 300 words on a person or topic covered in this unit. Student may choose from the topic suggestions below. However, the student may also choose another topic with the permission of their parent/teacher.

- Choose a passage or chapter in the Acts of the Apostles and write a summary of the passage with a few spiritual applications.

- Select one of the documents from the Apostolic Fathers. Read the document, and then provide an essay summarizing its main teachings.

- Write an essay defending the deity of the Son of God, Jesus Christ, using Scripture to establish your position.

- Choose one of the people covered in this unit. Write an essay explaining how he/she is a valuable example of Christian faith and life.

Unit 1 Optional Enrichment Projects

Choose one of these optional enrichment projects to complete Unit 1:

- **Presentation:** Create a 5-minute presentation on a person or event covered in this unit and present to your family or friends. Follow these steps:

    a. Introduce yourself and the subject you will talk about.
    b. Share some interesting facts you learned.
    c. End by stating your summary or opinion based on the facts of the topic.
    d. Thank your audience and invite them to ask any questions.

- **Geography:** Create a list of locations mentioned in this unit. Using online resources, create a map of a particular region (Mediterranean World, or a sublocation such as North Africa) and mark key persons and locations in this unit. Use your creativity and artistic skill to produce a map/poster board that is visually pleasing.

- **Timeline:** Using the timeline in the textbook and dates mentioned in the workbook, create your own timeline with poster board. Using internet resources, print pictures of key figures or locations and paste them onto your timeline.

- **Food:** Select a country or region mentioned in this unit. Research the most popular dishes from that particular country or region. Purchase the ingredients necessary and follow the recipe available in the cookbook or online resource and feed your family or friends!

- **Art:** Create a sketch of one of the persons covered in this unit. Or, create a sketch of a major event covered in this unit.

- **Music:** Find and learn a new hymn! Using a book hymnal available to you, or online sources (such as hymnary.org), search for a hymn that was written by one of the people covered in this unit (search for some of the key names covered in this unit). Learn how to sing the hymn with the family and explore its meaning together. If able, play the melody of the hymn on a musical instrument you have learned.

7. Missionary Expansion

TIMELINE AND LOCATION REVIEW

1. The Vandals besieged the town of Hippo in AD _____.

2. Augustine of Canterbury visited England around AD _____.

3. The monastery of Iona was founded in AD _____.

4. Clovis was baptized on Christmas Day, AD _____.

5. Alopen visited China around AD _____.

SHORT ANSWER

6. Who was the first writer to refer to the period of the Middle Ages as a period of darkness?

7. Name the Arian bishop who preached to the Germanic tribes.

8. What Visigoth king besieged Rome?

9. Name the Christian missionary who took the gospel to Ireland.

10. Who wrote the first church history of England?

11. Who did Gregory the Great send to the British Isles to evangelize?

12. During whose reign did the Franks embrace Christianity?

13. Who first translated the Bible into Slavonic?

14. Who defended the kingdom of Wessex against the Vikings?

15. According to tradition, who first took the gospel to India?

HEARING FROM GOD'S WORD

16. Read Isaiah 60:1-7. What does this prophecy say about the Gentile nations? How does this chapter historically demonstrate the fulfillment of this prophecy?

17. Read Psalm 67. What prayer or petition is found in verses 1-2? What promise is found in verse 7?

PRAYER

Now, take time to pray to God Almighty, asking that Jesus' kingdom would come, and Jesus' will would be done on earth as it is heaven.

- Pray for unreached people groups in the world, asking that the Lord would send missionaries to them so that they would be saved from their sins through faith in Jesus Christ.

- Pray that the Lord would raise up more missionaries, Bible translators, and teachers who would have a desire to spread the gospel.

- Choose one missionary or evangelist your church supports and spend time in prayer for their labors.

8. Christian Monasticism

PERSON MATCHING

1. Pachomius
2. Antony
3. Bede
4. Ulfilas
5. Benedict
6. Boniface

a. The first well-known monastic in Christian history

b. Arian bishop of the Goths

c. Missionary to the Germans and Frisians

d. Founder of communal monasticism

e. Father of English church history

f. Founder of monastery at Monte Cassino

SHORT ANSWER

7. Define asceticism.

8. Contrast eremitic monasticism with cenobitic monasticism.

9. Where did Pachomius found his monastic community?

10. In what village did Benedict grow up in?

11. What influential Rule did Benedict write?

12. What threefold pattern did Benedict require in his Rule?

13. List a few monastic orders that arose in the later Middle Ages mentioned in this chapter.

14. What was the title given to the leader of a monastery?

HEARING FROM GOD'S WORD

15. Read Colossians 2:20-23 and 1 Timothy 4:1-5. What warnings are found in these passages against externally imposed rules not required by God's Word?

16. Read Matthew 16:24-26. Our Lord teaches that the Christian life involves self-denial. Meditate for a time concerning how this command is applicable in your daily life at present. What sort of situations do you face regularly where you need to deny self?

PRAYER

Now, take time to pray to our Holy God, asking that He would work in you what is well pleasing in His sight.

- Give thanks to God for calling you out of a life of sin and self-seeking to live for Jesus Christ and for God's glory.

- Ask the Lord to make you increasingly holy, just as He is holy. Pray that you would be a young man/young woman filled with the fruit of the Holy Spirit and zealous for good works.

- Ask the Lord to give you the spiritual strength to deny yourself when the Lord Jesus calls you to give up something.

9. The Rise of Islam

TIMELINE AND LOCATION REVIEW

1. Muhammad was born around the year AD _____.

2. Muhammad was expelled from the city of Mecca in AD _____.

3. Charles Martel drove back the Muslims in the battle of _____.

4. Pope Urban II called for the first crusade at the Council of Clermont in AD _____.

5. The city of Acre fell to the Muslims in AD _____.

6. John the Theologian lived under Muslim rule in _____.

SHORT ANSWER

7. Name the false god of Islam.

8. Name the most important city which Muslims are to make a pilgrimage to at least once in their lifetime.

9. What false doctrines are taught in Surah 4 of the Qur'an?

10. Name the "Five Pillars" of Islam.

11. What Latin phrase was chanted after Pope Urban called for the first crusade?

12. Name the English King who participated in the Third Crusade.

13. What missionary from the 1200s made an effort to reach the Muslim world with the gospel?

14. What theologian defended Christianity against Muslim teaching and wrote the book *The Orthodox Faith*?

HEARING FROM GOD'S WORD

15. Read 2 Corinthians 10:3-5. What does Paul mean when he says our weapons are "not carnal?" According to this passage, how do we wage the Christian warfare?

16. Read 1 Peter 3:13-15. In what manner should we give a defense for our Christian hope? What sort of characteristics does Peter list?

PRAYER

Now, take time to pray to our Father in Heaven, asking that He would care for His people all over the world.

- Using an online resource such as Voice of the Martyrs, Open Doors, or Operation World, select one Muslim-majority country to pray for. Ask the Lord to advance the gospel in that land, to defeat false religion, and to bring about conversions of the Muslim population in that land.

- Pray for opportunities you may have with people of other religions in your life. Ask the Lord to open doors whereby you can share the hope you have received through the gospel.

10. The Development of the Papacy

PERSON MATCHING

1. Innocent III
2. Stephen I
3. Leo I
4. Gregory I
5. Lorenzo Valla
6. Gregory VII
7. Henry IV
8. Frederick Barbarossa

a. First bishop of Rome to claim that the Apostle Peter spoke directly through him

b. Previous to his papacy, he was known as Hildebrand

c. First bishop of Rome to claim authority over other bishops

d. Among the most humble holders of the office of bishop of Rome

e. A king who begged the Pope for mercy during the winter at Canossa

f. Pope who exercised the greatest degree of authority of all time

g. Renaissance writer who demonstrated that the Donation of Constantine was a forgery

h. Holy Roman Emperor who fought in the Crusades

SHORT ANSWER

9. Define the word "vicar" as applied to the Pope.

10. What did Gregory I say about those who claimed the title universal bishop?

11. What did the document *The Donation of Constantine* claim?

12. Who was among the most disreputable and criminal of all popes mentioned in this chapter?

13. What did the Cluniac reformers set out to do as summarized in this chapter?

14. In Hildebrand's decree concerning the papacy, what claims did he make?

15. What happened at the Castle of Canossa?

HEARING FROM GOD'S WORD

16. Read Mark 10:42-45. What example of leadership did our Lord Jesus Christ set? How does Gentile (worldly) leadership differ from those who lead according to the example of Christ?

17. Read Philippians 2:3-4. What two patterns of behavior does Paul contrast in these verses?

PRAYER

Now, spend time in prayer before the Lord Almighty, asking that He would grant you to walk in the humble pattern of the Lord Jesus Christ.

- Thank the Lord for the humble, sacrificial service of Jesus Christ, who humbled himself to the death on the cross, securing the way of your salvation.

- Ask the Lord to grant you true humility, so that you would no longer seek out your own interests, but that you would grow to be more of a servant, sacrificially giving yourself to others.

- Ask the Lord to bless your church with the grace of humility.

11. Schism in the Church

TIMELINE MATCHING

1. The Second Council of Nicaea   a. 451

2. The Council of Constantinople   b. 325

3. The Synod of Toledo   c. 381

4. The First Council of Nicaea   d. 787

5. The Great Schism   e. 589

6. The Council of Chalcedon   f. 1054

SHORT ANSWER

7. What does the word "schism" mean?

8. What happened in the Great Schism?

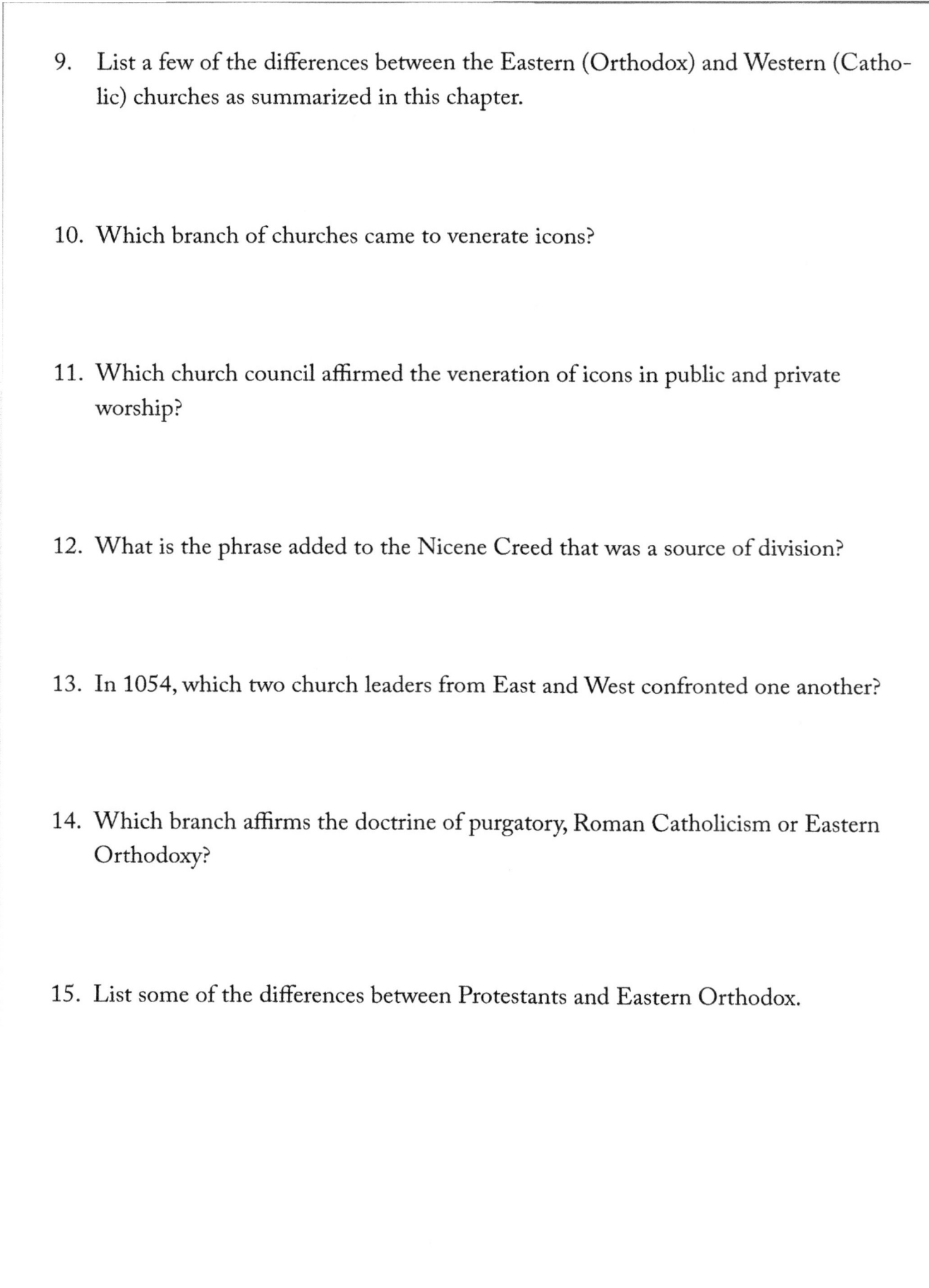

9. List a few of the differences between the Eastern (Orthodox) and Western (Catholic) churches as summarized in this chapter.

10. Which branch of churches came to venerate icons?

11. Which church council affirmed the veneration of icons in public and private worship?

12. What is the phrase added to the Nicene Creed that was a source of division?

13. In 1054, which two church leaders from East and West confronted one another?

14. Which branch affirms the doctrine of purgatory, Roman Catholicism or Eastern Orthodoxy?

15. List some of the differences between Protestants and Eastern Orthodox.

HEARING FROM GOD'S WORD

16. Read Ephesians 4:1-3. If we will maintain the unity of Christ's church, what sort of spiritual characteristics must we walk in?

17. Read 1 Corinthians 11:18-19. According to this passage, what is one of God's purposes in permitting divisions to occur within the church?

PRAYER

Now, take time in prayer to ask the Lord to bless Christ's church with unity.

- Pray that the Lord would grow you in humility, gentleness, and longsuffering so that you would be better equipped to be a unity-minded, and unity-pursuing member of your church.

- Ask the Lord to grow the unity of faith and love in your local congregation.

- Pray that God would grow the unity of Christ's church in your local area between local assemblies who preach the Bible and faithfully proclaim the gospel of Jesus Christ.

Unit 2 Exam: The Early Middle Ages

Total: 40 Points

TIMELINE MATCHING

1. The Council of Chalcedon   a. 1095

2. Muhammad born   b. 1291

3. Pope Urban II calls for the First Crusade   c. 325

4. The Synod of Toledo   d. 787

5. The City of Acre falls to the Muslims   e. 451

6. The First Council of Nicaea   f. 635

7. The Great Schism   g. 570

8. The Second Council of Nicaea   h. 430

9. Alopen visits China   i. 589

10. The Vandals besiege Hippo   j. 1054

PERSON MATCHING

11. Boniface

12. Bede

13. Frederick Barbarossa

14. Gregory VII

15. Antony

16. Henry IV

17. Gregory I

18. Innocent III

19. John of Damascus

20. Muhammad

a. Previous to his papacy, he was known as Hildebrand

b. A king who begged the Pope for mercy during the winter at Canossa

c. Among the most humble holders of the office of bishop of Rome

d. Holy Roman Emperor who fought in the Crusades

e. Pope who exercised the greatest degree of authority of all time

f. Missionary to the Germans and Frisians

g. Theologian who wrote *The Orthodox Faith*

h. Father of English church history

i. Founder of Islam

j. The first well-known monastic in Christian history

MULTIPLE CHOICE

21. What political and military leader won a victory over the Muslims at the Battle of Tours?

    A. Clovis
    B. Charlemagne
    C. Charles Martel
    D. Muhammad

22. Which church council affirmed the veneration of icons?

    A. The First Council of Nicaea
    B. The Second Council of Nicaea
    C. The Council of Chalcedon
    D. The Synod of Toledo

23. Name the English king who participated in the Third Crusade

    A. Frederick Barbarossa
    B. John
    C. Phillip II
    D. Richard

24. What is the most important city for Muslims?

    A. Mecca
    B. Medina
    C. Jerusalem
    D. Damascus

25. In what town did Benedict grow up?

    A. Assisi
    B. Nursia
    C. Monte Cassino
    D. Clairvaux

26. What heresy states that human beings are NOT born with a depraved, sinful condition inherited from Adam?

    A. Arianism
    B. Sabellianism
    C. Pelagianism
    D. Eutychianism

27. According to tradition, which apostle first took the Gospel to India?

    A. John
    B. Peter
    C. Mark
    D. Thomas

28. Which writer determined that the Donation of Constantine was a forgery?

    A. Petrarch
    B. Lorenzo Valla
    C. Bede
    D. Pachomius

29. At what church council was the *Filioque* clause added to the Nicene Creed?

    A. The Council of Constantinople
    B. The Synod of Toledo
    C. The Council of Chalcedon
    D. The Second Council of Nicaea

30. Which pope stated "Whosoever calls himself universal priest, or desires to be called so, was the forerunner of Antichrist."
    A. Innocent III
    B. Gregory VII
    C. Gregory I
    D. Leo I

31. Which pope is named in the Donation of Constantine?
    A. Leo I
    B. Stephen
    C. Innocent II
    D. Sylvester

32. In what region did Pachomius found his monastic community?
    A. Italy
    B. Egypt
    C. Palestine
    D. Turkey

33. Name the king who sacked Rome in AD 410.
    A. Alaric
    B. Clovis
    C. Ulfilas
    D. Charles Martel

34. What missionary was sent by Gregory to take the Gospel to Great Britain?
    A. Boniface
    B. Augustine
    C. Clovis
    D. Patrick

35. Irenaeus wrote against which heretical group in *Against Heresies*?
    A. Arianism
    B. Sabellianism
    C. Gnosticism
    D. Pelagianism

36. Who wrote *The City of God*?
    A. Ambrose
    B. Origen
    C. Athanasius
    D. Augustine

37. The "Great Persecution" occurred during the reign of which Emperor?
    A. Diocletian
    B. Domitian
    C. Nero
    D. Decius

38. Which of these documents served as an apology, or defense, of the Christian faith?

    A. *The Shepherd of Hermas*
    B. *The Martyrdom of Polycarp*
    C. *The Letter to Diognetus*
    D. *The Didache*

39. Which of these pillars of the "Five Pillars of Islam" is the basic creed of Islam?

    A. The *Salah*
    B. The *Zakah*
    C. *Sawm*
    D. The *Shahadah*

40. Who cut down a sacred oak in defiance of false religion?

    A. Boniface
    B. Patrick
    C. Augustine
    D. Ulfilas

Unit 2 Essay: The Early Middle Ages

Write an essay of at least 300 words on a person or topic covered in this unit. Student may choose from the topic suggestions below. However, the student may also choose another topic with the permission of their parent/teacher.

- Read the *Rule of St. Benedict* (available in print form or online). In an essay, summarize aspects of the Rule that are also found in Holy Scripture. Identify and explain parts of the *Rule* that are not rules found in Scripture.

- Research differences of belief between Islam and Christianity (online resources include CARM.org, the Christian Apologetics and Research ministry) and explain the most important differences between Christian and Muslim beliefs.

- Choose one missionary covered in this chapter and write a summary of their life.

- Write an essay that brings together at least three Scripture passages on unity in the church. Explain the meaning of these passages and give a few applications for each passage on how a Christian can pursue unity.

Unit 2 Optional Enrichment Projects

Choose one of these optional enrichment projects to complete Unit 2:

- **Presentation:** Create a 5-minute presentation on a person or event covered in this unit and present to your family or friends. Follow these steps:
    a. Introduce yourself and the subject you will talk about.
    b. Share some interesting facts you learned.
    c. End by stating your summary or opinion based on the facts of the topic.
    d. Thank your audience and invite them to ask any questions.

- **Geography:** Create a list of locations mentioned in this unit. Using online resources, create a map of a particular region (Mediterranean World, or a sublocation such as Italy) and mark key persons and locations in this unit. Use your creativity and artistic skill to produce a map/poster board that is visually pleasing.

- **Timeline:** Using the timeline in the textbook and dates mentioned in the workbook, create your own timeline with poster board. Using internet resources, print pictures of key figures or locations and paste them onto your timeline.

- **Food:** Select a country or region mentioned in this unit. Research the most popular dishes from that particular country or region. Purchase the ingredients necessary and follow the recipe available in the cookbook or online resource and feed your family or friends!

- **Art:** Create a sketch of one of the persons covered in this unit. Or, create a sketch of a major event covered in this unit.

- **Music:** Find and learn a new hymn! Using a book hymnal available to you, or online sources (such as hymnary.org), search for a hymn that was written by one of the people covered in this unit (search for some of the key names covered in this unit), or a hymn written in this period of church history. Learn how to sing the hymn with the family and explore its meaning together. If able, play the melody of the hymn on a musical instrument you have learned.

12. Universities and Scholasticism

PERSON MATCHING

1. Anselm
2. Thomas Aquinas
3. Albertus Magnus
4. Aristotle
5. Peter Lombard
6. Cardinal Humbert
7. Lorenzo Valla
8. Pachomius

a. Ancient Greek philosopher
b. Founder of communal Monasticism
c. Representative of the Western church who visited Constantinople
d. Wrote *Summa Theologica*
e. Taught Thomas Aquinas
f. Archbishop of Canterbury who wrote on the atonement
g. Renaissance writer who demonstrated that the Donation of Constantine was a forgery
h. Wrote *The Sentences*

SHORT ANSWER

9. What was the first university in Europe?

10. What two forms of teaching occurred in universities?

11. What sort of problems resulted from having many young people living together without parental supervision at the universities?

12. What university was well known as a source of theological teaching and development?

13. Which Greek philosopher had a significant influence on the development of Scholastic theology?

14. What book on the atonement did Anselm write?

15. What distinction between sins did Thomas Aquinas teach in his writings?

HEARING FROM GOD'S WORD

16. Read 1 Corinthians 8:1-3. What warning does Paul give about knowledge in this passage?

17. Read Proverbs 30:1-6. What does Agur confess in this passage? What does this passage teach us about humility in our knowledge?

PRAYER

Now, pray to the Lord who is infinite in knowledge, wisdom, and understanding.

- Praise God for His unsearchable wisdom and judgments. Give Him glory for His infinite knowledge and perfect wisdom.

- Ask the Lord to give you a humble heart so that as you grow in knowledge, you will also grow in humility.

- Pray that you would be a humble and hungry student of God's Word growing in the grace and knowledge of Jesus Christ.

13. Monasticism in the Middle Ages

PERSON MATCHING

1. Bernard of Clairvaux
2. Dominic of Caleruega
3. Francis of Assisi
4. Raymond Lull
5. Rudolf
6. Benedict of Nursia

a. Founded the Dominican order
b. Early missionary to Muslims
c. German monk who urged European Christians to rid Europe of the Jews
d. Wrote "Jesus, Thou Joy of Loving Hearts"
e. Founded a monastery at Monte Cassino
f. Wrote "All Creatures of Our God and King"

SHORT ANSWER

7. Which church council forbade the creation of new monastic orders? When did it occur?

8. Where was the first monastery of the Cistercians founded?

9. What does the word "Clairvaux" mean?

10. What warfare endeavor did Bernard support in his preaching?

11. When did the Inquisition against the Cathars begin?

12. Which monastic rule did the Dominicans adopt for their use?

13. What does the term "mendicant" mean?

14. What did Philip Schaff have to say about monasticism in the Middle Ages, as quoted near the end of this chapter?

HEARING FROM GOD'S WORD

15. Read 1 Timothy 6:6-8. Review Paul's words and explain, based on what you have learned about monasticism, what aspects of monasticism were edifying and biblical in nature vs. those elements that were not as faithful to Scripture.

PRAYER

Now, pray to our Holy God, asking that He would consecrate you to a life of holiness and Christian service.

- Give thanks to the Lord for calling us out of a life of sin and death and into His church and calling us saints (holy ones).

- Ask that the Lord would grow you in holiness.

- Pray that God would show you how can you through love serve others, and live a life unspotted from the world.

14. The Papal Schism and the Conciliar Movement

TIMELINE MATCHING

1. The papal bull *Unam Sanctum* is issued   a. 1198-1215

2. The Babylonian Captivity of the Papacy (the Avignon Papacy)   b. 1414-1418

3. The papacy of Innocent III   c. 1431

4. The Council of Pisa   d. 1301

5. The Council of Constance   e. 1409

6. The Council of Basel   f. 1309-1377

SHORT ANSWER

7. What did the bull *Unam Sanctum* declare was absolutely necessary for salvation?

8. Around what date did the Black Death begin in Europe?

9. When the papacy returned to Rome, who was the first pope of that period?

10. Name some of the theologians who advocated for the Conciliar movement.

11. Which pope attempted to stop the Council of Basel?

12. Which reformer of the Middle Ages was executed at the Council of Constance?

HEARING FROM GOD'S WORD

13. Read 1 Peter 5:1-4. What does Peter call faithful elders to be? How are they to care for God's people? How did the popes described in this chapter fall short of Peter's call for church leaders?

14. Read 1 Corinthians 3:3-4. According to this passage, what is one characteristic of fleshly, immature behavior?

PRAYER

Now, take time to pray to the God of heaven, asking that He would grant the blessings of unity to the church of Christ.

- Give thanks to God for faithful church shepherds. Pray for your pastor/elders asking that the Lord would grow them as faithful servants, and as godly examples to the flock.

- Pray for an increase of faithful shepherds for the church, so that the church would be strengthened for additional ministry. Ask God to provide qualified, godly, and called men to the work of pastoral ministry.

15. Reform Efforts in the Middle Ages

PERSON MATCHING

1. Innocent III
2. John Wycliffe
3. Peter Waldo
4. John Huss
5. John of Gaunt
6. Sir John Oldcastle
7. King Wenceslas
8. Gregory XI

a. Reformer who taught at Oxford University
b. Founder of the Waldensian movement
c. First Pope who authorized the persecution and killing of the Waldensians
d. Significant supporter of John Wycliffe
e. King of Bohemia
f. Reform preacher in Prague
g. Pope who summoned John Wycliffe to Rome
h. Well-known Lollard who was executed

SHORT ANSWER

9. Where did the Waldensian movement originate from?

10. What church council declared the Waldensians to be heretics? When did it occur?

11. What Bible passage did Waldensians use to support their view that Christians should never take oaths?

12. In what region did the Waldensians hide from persecution?

13. What significant publication was completed in 1395?

14. What did Wycliffe's followers become known as?

15. What did Huss' followers become known as?

HEARING FROM GOD'S WORD

16. Read Matthew 10:27-28. What wrong fear does Jesus warn us against? What is the difference between the power of men and the power of God? What are some examples from this chapter of men who had the right kind of fear?

PRAYER

Now, take time to seek the face of the Lord in prayer.

- Give thanks to God for His infallible revelation, the Scriptures. Give thanks to God for the clarity of the Bible, and for its value in guiding us in the Christian life.

- Ask the Lord to bring a restored faithfulness to the Bible in the church in your country or state.

- Pray for your local church that it would reform those areas of doctrine or practice that are not faithful to God's Word.

Unit 3 Exam: The Late Middle Ages

Total: 40 Points

TIMELINE MATCHING

1. The Council of Constance   a. 589

2. The papacy of Innocent III   b. 1309-1377

3. The Synod of Toledo   c. 1054

4. The Great Schism   d. 570

5. The Babylonian Captivity of the Papacy (the Avignon Papacy)   e. 1409

6. Muhammad born   f. 1414-1418

7. Pope Urban II calls for the First Crusade   g. 1073-1085

8. The Council of Pisa   h. 1198-1215

9. The papacy of Gregory VII   i. 635

10. Alopen visits China   j. 1095

PERSON MATCHING

11. Anselm

12. Peter Lombard

13. Bernard of Clairvaux

14. John Wycliffe

15. Thomas Aquinas

16. John Huss

17. Raymond Lull

18. Dominic of Caleruega

19. Albertus Magnus

20. Sir John Oldcastle

a. Reformer who taught at Oxford University

b. Early missionary to Muslims

c. Wrote *The Sentences*

d. Taught Thomas Aquinas

e. Reform preacher in Prague

f. Well-known Lollard who was executed

g. Archbishop of Canterbury who wrote on the atonement

h. Wrote *Summa Theologica*

i. Wrote "Jesus, Thou Joy of Loving Hearts"

j. Founded the Dominican order

MULTIPLE CHOICE

21. Who wrote *Cur Deus Homo*?

    A. Thomas Aquinas
    B. Anselm
    C. Peter Lombard
    D. Albertus Magnus

22. Which monastic rule did the Dominicans adopt?

    A. The Rule of St. Benedict
    B. The Rule of St. Francis
    C. The Rule of St. Augustine
    D. The Rule of St. Basil

23. At what council was John Huss executed?

    A. The Council of Pisa
    B. The Council of Constance
    C. The Council of Basel
    D. The Council of Constantinople

24. Where did the Waldensians take refuge amid persecution?

    A. Piedmont
    B. Lyons
    C. Canossa
    D. Prague

25. Whose philosophy did Thomas Aquinas revive and integrate into his theology?

    A. Socrates
    B. Plato
    C. Demosthenes
    D. Aristotle

26. In what place did the Waldensian movement originate?

    A. London
    B. Lyons
    C. Paris
    D. Rome

27. Who formulated the ontological argument for God's existence?

    A. Albertus Magnus
    B. Thomas Aquinas
    C. Anselm
    D. Peter Lombard

28. Which of these orders was a "Mendicant" (begging) order?

    A. Benedictine
    B. Franciscan
    C. Cistercian
    D. Cluniac

29. What is the most important city for Muslims?

    A. Mecca
    B. Medina
    C. Jerusalem
    D. Damascus

30. Martyred in Lyons during the reign of Emperor Marcus Aurelius

    A. Polycarp
    B. Ignatius
    C. Stephen
    D. Blandina

31. According to tradition, which apostle first took the Gospel to India?

    A. John
    B. Peter
    C. Mark
    D. Thomas

32. Clovis was baptized on Christmas Day in what year?

    A. 496
    B. 732
    C. 622
    D. 570

33. What heresy states that human beings are NOT born with a depraved, sinful condition inherited from Adam?

    A. Arianism
    B. Sabellianism
    C. Pelagianism
    D. Eutychianism

34. Served as Bishop of Hippo

    A. Tertullian
    B. Origen
    C. Augustine
    D. Irenaeus

35. Which church council affirmed the veneration of icons?

    A. The First Council of Nicaea
    B. The Second Council of Nicaea
    C. The Council of Chalcedon
    D. The Synod of Toledo

36. Constantine defeated who at the Battle of Milvian Bridge?

    A. Galerius
    B. Maxentius
    C. Licinius
    D. Diocletian

37. Which pope stated "Whosoever calls himself universal priest, or desires to be called so, was the forerunner of Antichrist."

    A. Innocent III
    B. Gregory VII
    C. Gregory I
    D. Leo I

38. What was the first university founded in Europe?

    A. University of Bologna
    B. University of Oxford
    C. University of Paris
    D. University of Orleans

39. Name the King who sacked Rome in AD 410.

    A. Alaric
    B. Clovis
    C. Ulfilas
    D. Charles Martel

40. Name the English King who participated in the Third Crusade

    A. Frederick Barbarossa
    B. John
    C. Phillip II
    D. Richard the Lionhearted

Unit 3 Essay: The Late Middle Ages

Write an essay of at least 300 words on a person or topic covered in this unit. Student may choose from the topic suggestions below. However, the student may also choose another topic with the permission of their parent/teacher.

- Write an essay explaining the differences in belief between the Waldensians and Cathars (Albigensians).

- Write an essay recounting the major events in the life of John Wycliffe or John Huss.

- Using online or print resources, read a sermon from Bernard of Clairvaux. Summarize in an essay what the sermon is about and detail which Scripture Bernard references.

- Using Holy Scripture, and what you have learned about monasticism in this course so far, write an essay evaluating monasticism.

Unit 3 Optional Enrichment Projects

Choose one of these optional enrichment projects to complete Unit 3:

- **Presentation:** Create a 5-minute presentation on a person or event covered in this unit and present to your family or friends. Follow these steps:

    a. Introduce yourself and the subject you will talk about.
    b. Share some interesting facts you learned.
    c. End by stating your summary or opinion based on the facts of the topic.
    d. Thank your audience and invite them to ask any questions.

- **Geography:** Create a list of locations mentioned in this unit. Using online resources, create a map of a particular region (Mediterranean World, or a sublocation such as Italy) and mark key persons and locations in this unit. Use your creativity and artistic skill to produce a map/poster board that is visually pleasing.

- **Timeline:** Using the timeline in the textbook and dates mentioned in the workbook, create your own timeline with poster board. Using internet resources, print pictures of key figures or locations and paste them onto your timeline.

- **Food:** Select a country or region mentioned in this unit. Research the most popular dishes from that particular country or region. Purchase the ingredients necessary and follow the recipe available in the cookbook or online resource and feed your family or friends!

- **Art:** Create a sketch of one of the persons covered in this unit. Or, create a sketch of a major event covered in this unit.

- **Music:** Find and learn a new hymn! Using a book hymnal available to you, or online sources (such as hymnary.org), search for a hymn that was written by one of the people covered in this unit (search for some of the key names covered in this unit), or a hymn written in this period of church history. Learn how to sing the hymn with the family and explore its meaning together. If able, play the melody of the hymn on a musical instrument you have learned.

16. The Dawn of the Reformation

TIMELINE MATCHING

1. Gutenberg's invention of the movable type printing press   a. 1453

2. Constantinople falls to the Turks   b. 1492

3. The *Gutenberg Bible* printed   c. 1516

4. Christopher Columbus discovers the Americas   d. 1455

5. Erasmus publishes his *Novum Instrumentum* (Greek New Testament)   e. 1414-1418

6. The Protestant Reformation begins   f. 1439

7. The Council of Constance   g. 1054

8. The Great Schism   h. 1517

SHORT ANSWER

9. How did the invention of the movable type printing press aid the cause of the Reformation?

10. What does *ad Fontes* mean?

11. What man was responsible for the revival of the study of Hebrew?

12. What was contained in Erasmus' *Novum Instrumentum*?

13. Which pope did Erasmus critique in his satirical writings as detailed in this chapter?

PRAYER

Now, take time to give thanks to the Lord for the light of His Word!

- Give thanks to God for giving us the Bible which has been providentially preserved, and is the infallible Word of God.

- Give thanks to the Lord for bringing light to His church through the events of the Protestant Reformation.

- Ask the Lord to bring about an increase of biblical knowledge among the people of your country. Pray that more and more people would read and love the Word of God.

17. The Reformation in Germany

TIMELINE AND LOCATION REVIEW

1. Martin Luther encountered a lightning storm on his way home in AD _____.

2. Martin Luther entered the Augustinian monastery at _____.

3. Luther reached Rome on Christmas Eve in AD _____.

4. Luther posted his 95 Theses in AD _____.

5. Luther taught at the University of _____.

6. Luther was hidden in the Castle at _____.

7. Luther defended his doctrine in 1521 at the Diet of _____.

SHORT ANSWER

8. What staircase did Luther ascend while visiting Rome?

9. What subject did Luther teach at the University of Wittenberg?

10. What critical discovery did Luther make in 1519 while studying Romans?

11. What indulgence preacher passed near Wittenberg selling indulgences?

12. Who did Martin Luther debate in 1519?

13. What important task did Luther accomplish while in hiding after the Diet of Worms?

14. Where did Martin Luther live with his wife and children?

15. What is Luther's most well-known hymn?

HEARING FROM GOD'S WORD

16. Read Romans 1:16-17. How does Paul describe the gospel in these verses? How does this give us confidence when we share the gospel with others?

PRAYER

Now, take time to pray to the God of grace.

- Give thanks to God for the power of the gospel and how that power has changed your life.

- Give thanks to God for the blessing of justification, being declared righteous in God's sight because of the righteousness of our Savior Jesus Christ.

- Give thanks to the Lord for raising up faithful servants who boldly proclaimed the truth of the gospel, even though they were severely opposed by the world.

- Pray for your pastor/elders to faithfully proclaim the gospel of God's grace, and that the Lord would prosper the ministry of the Word.

18. The Swiss Reformation in Zurich

PERSON MATCHING

1. Desiderius Erasmus
2. Konrad Grebel
3. Christopher Froschauer
4. Anna Reinhart
5. Ulrich Zwingli
6. Martin Luther
7. Heinrich Bullinger
8. Bernhardin Sanson

a. Ulrich Zwingli's wife
b. Met with Zwingli at Marburg
c. Preacher at the Grossmünster
d. Published an edition of the Greek New Testament in 1516
e. Zwingli's successor in Zurich
f. One of the founders of the Anabaptist movement
g. The printer in Zurich
h. Franciscan preacher who sold indulgences

SHORT ANSWER

9. Before Zwingli served as a pastor in Zurich, in what other towns did Zwingli minister?

10. Which humanist writer influenced Zwingli?

11. What trial afflicted Zurich during the first year of Zwingli's ministry there?

12. Why was the sausage feast in March 1522 so controversial?

13. Which Anabaptist leader was executed on February 5, 1527?

14. What theological disagreement was left unresolved at the Marburg Colloquy?

15. How did Zwingli die?

HEARING FROM GOD'S WORD

16. Read 1 Timothy 4:1-2. What commands does Paul give Timothy in this passage? What sort of words does Paul use to describe preaching?

17. Read Exodus 20:4-6. How did Zwingli and other reformers in Zurich understand the application of this commandment? Describe some important applications of this commandment in the modern day.

PRAYER

Now, take time to pray to the Lord, Your Father in Heaven.

- Ask the Lord to grant pure worship in His church, and that your local church would be a place where faithful preaching and God-centered worship is upheld.

- Ask the Lord to give you wisdom when it comes to disagreements over minor matters between fellow Christians. Ask the Lord to grow you in seeking unity, and in always speaking the truth in love.

19. The Anabaptist Movement

TIMELINE MATCHING

1. Felix Manz executed   a. 1525

2. A public debate occurs in Zurich over the matter of infant baptism   b. 1537

3. Anabaptist radicals take over Münster   c. 1540

4. Menno Simons becomes a pastor in Groningen   d. 1527

5. Menno Simons writes *The Foundation of Christian Doctrine*   e. 1535

6. The Münster revolt is ended   f. 1534

SHORT ANSWER

7. What are the three streams of the Protestant Reformation described in this chapter?

8. Where did the Anabaptist movement have its beginnings?

9. What was the earliest form of baptismal mode used by the Anabaptists?

10. Who coined the term "Anabaptist"?

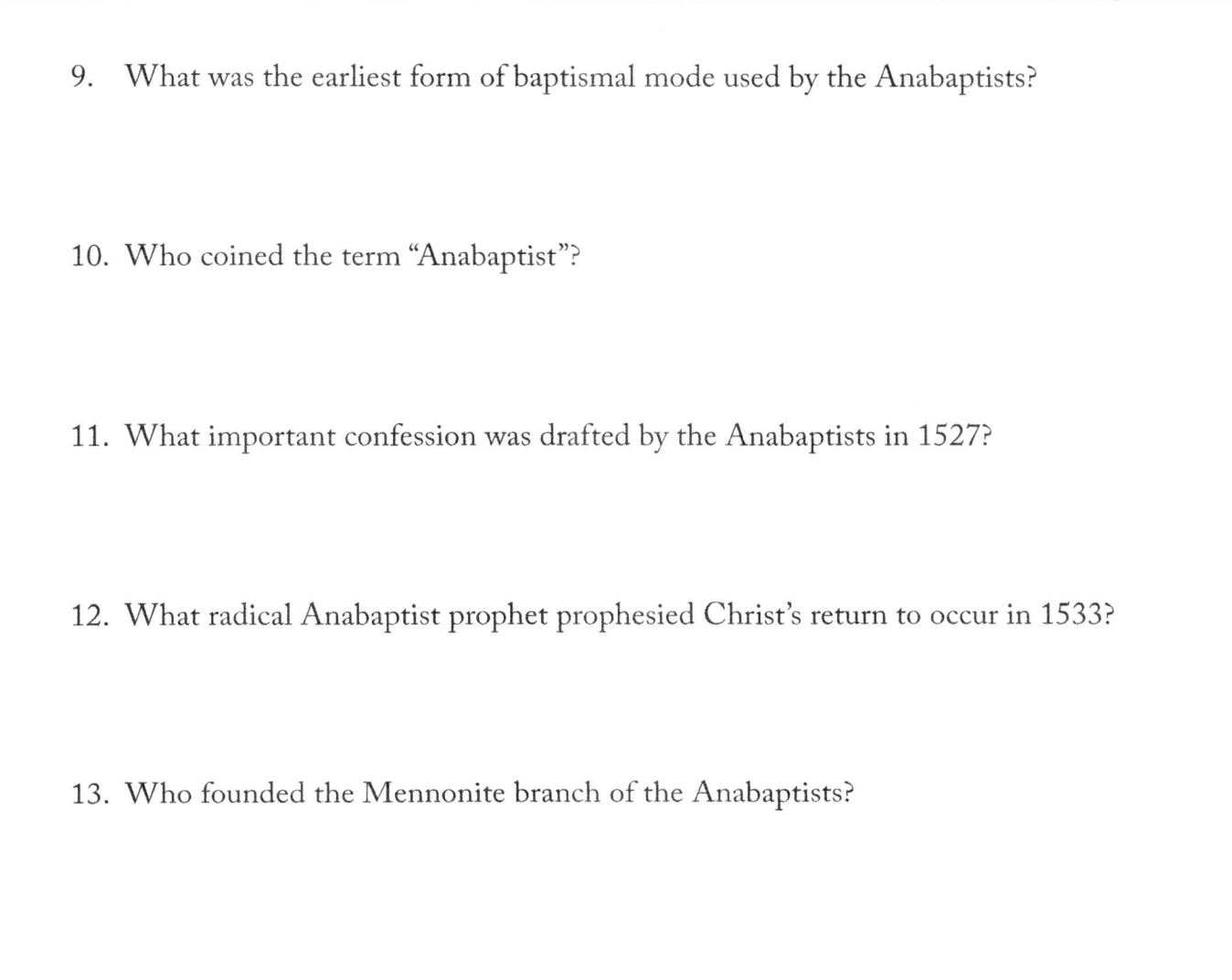

11. What important confession was drafted by the Anabaptists in 1527?

12. What radical Anabaptist prophet prophesied Christ's return to occur in 1533?

13. Who founded the Mennonite branch of the Anabaptists?

HEARING FROM GOD'S WORD

14. Read James 3:17-18. Consider James' instructions on peacemaking by walking in heavenly wisdom. In what ways do you think the people of Zurich failed to resolve the situation in a godly manner?

15. Read Deuteronomy 18:20-22. What instruction does this passage give us in analyzing those who claim the gift of prophecy?

PRAYER

Now, take time to pray to the Lord.

- Ask the Lord to grant you the wisdom from above; that you would be a peaceable, gentle, and merciful person when you deal with disagreements.

- Ask the Lord to bless your local church with unity, peace, and joy in the Holy Spirit.

- Pray that God would grow your understanding of appreciation for of some of His gifts to the church including baptism and the Lord's Supper, which are often matters of division between Christian believers.

20. The Reformation in Geneva

PERSON MATCHING

1. Heinrich Bullinger
2. John Calvin
3. Martin Bucer
4. Michael Servetus
5. William Farel
6. John Knox
7. Louis du Tillet
8. Francis I

a. Reformer who urged Calvin to come and minister in Geneva

b. Reformer in Strasbourg and mentor to John Calvin

c. Scottish reformer

d. Zwingli's successor in Zurich

e. Calvin wrote him a letter defending Protestantism

f. Wrote *Institutes of the Christian Religion*

g. Medical doctor who espoused heresy

h. Calvin spent time in his home studying the Bible and the church fathers

SHORT ANSWER

9. What was the name of Calvin's friend at the University of Paris?

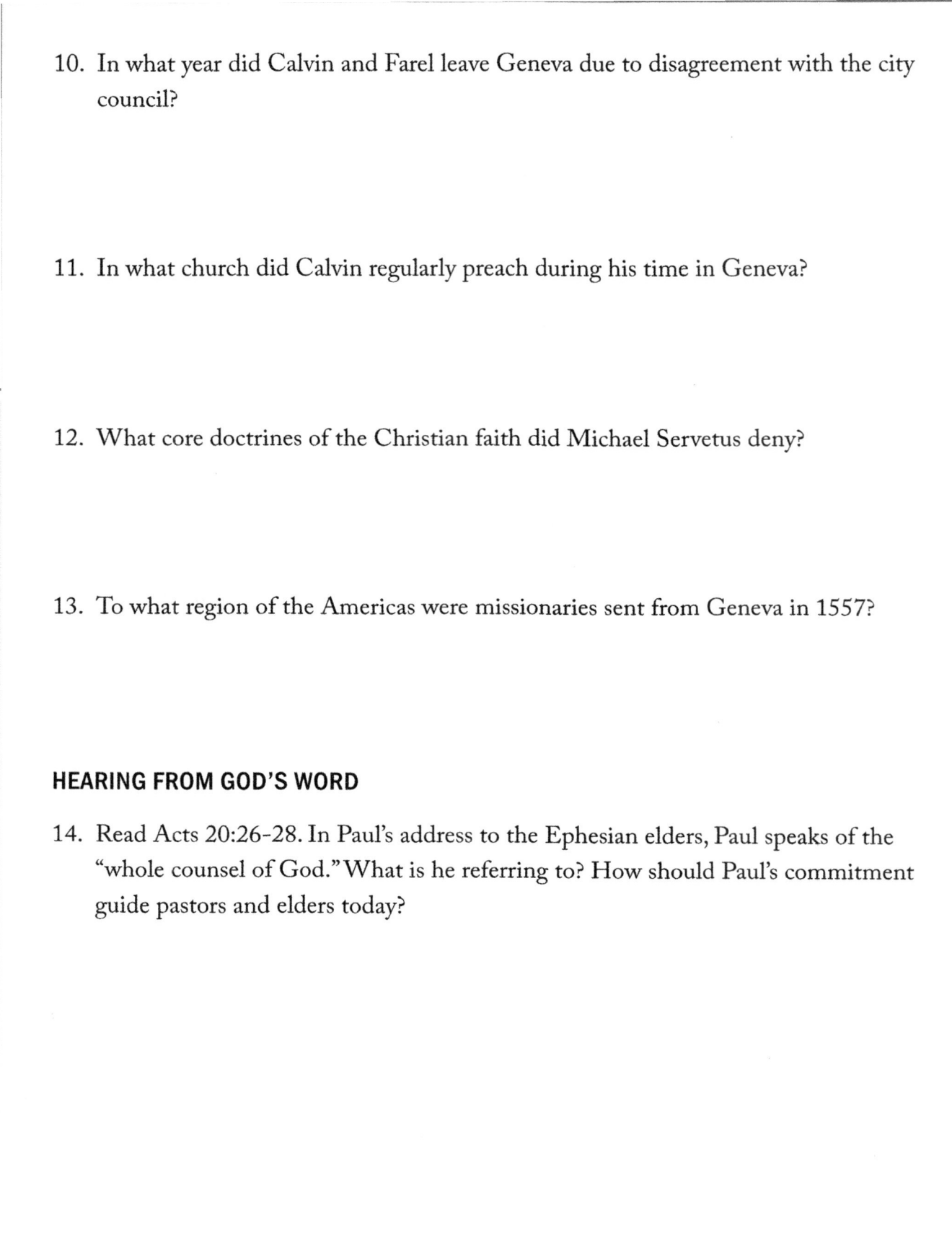

10. In what year did Calvin and Farel leave Geneva due to disagreement with the city council?

11. In what church did Calvin regularly preach during his time in Geneva?

12. What core doctrines of the Christian faith did Michael Servetus deny?

13. To what region of the Americas were missionaries sent from Geneva in 1557?

HEARING FROM GOD'S WORD

14. Read Acts 20:26-28. In Paul's address to the Ephesian elders, Paul speaks of the "whole counsel of God." What is he referring to? How should Paul's commitment guide pastors and elders today?

15. Read Acts 6:1-7. For what purpose were the seven men (deacons) in Acts 6 set aside? How did they assist the apostles? What did the apostles give their focused attention to?

PRAYER

Now, take time to give thanks to God, and to ask the Lord for His blessings.

- Give thanks to God for faithful preachers and teachers who shepherd God's people to understand His Word and to practice it.

- Thank the Lord for the power of His Holy Word, which is sharper than a two-edged sword, and is a source of encouragement and hope.

- Ask the Lord to raise up faithful teachers who will preach the whole counsel of God.

21. William Tyndale and the English Bible

TIMELINE MATCHING

1. Tyndale's first edition of the English New Testament published   a. 1535

2. The Coverdale Bible published   b. 1536

3. Tyndale's second edition of the English New Testament published   c. 1538

4. Tyndale is executed   d. 1526

5. King Henry VIII issues a decree that every church should have an English Bible   e. 1611

6. The English Authorised Version published   f. 1534

SHORT ANSWER

7. Approximately how much of Tyndale's English translation of the New Testament is retained in the English Authorised Version (KJV)?

8. To which bishop of London did Tyndale go to seek permission to translate the New Testament into English and to publish it?

9. In what city did Tyndale successfully publish his first edition of the English New Testament?

10. What was the effect of Archbishop William Warham's attempt to purchase all the copies of Tyndale's English New Testament?

11. Who betrayed William Tyndale to the authorities?

12. What was Tyndale's dying prayer?

HEARING FROM GOD'S WORD

13. Read Psalm 119:14-16 and Psalm 19:10-11. What do these passages say about the value we should place upon God's Word?

14. Read Jeremiah 23:29. What does this verse say about the power of God's word? Reflect upon some ways in which the power of God's Word has been at work in your church and family. List some ways in which you have seen the power of God evident through the Bible.

PRAYER

Now, take time to pray to the Lord, giving thanks for the blessing of His Holy Word.

- Thank the Lord for the inspiration and preservation of the Holy Scriptures throughout the centuries.

- Thank the Lord for providing you access to the written Word, so that you can read it, meditate upon it, and put it into practice.

- Pray for the work of Bible translators all over the world, that the Lord would bring about the translation of the Bible into every spoken language of the world.

22. The Reformation in England

TIMELINE AND LOCATION REVIEW

1. Thomas Cranmer became Archbishop of Canterbury in AD _____.

2. The first edition of the *Book of Common Prayer* was issued in AD _____.

3. Edward VI died in AD _____.

4. Thomas Cranmer was executed in AD _____.

5. Elizabeth I reigned from AD _____ to AD _____.

6. Thomas Cranmer was executed in the town of _____.

SHORT ANSWER

7. Why was King Henry VIII dissatisfied with his first wife, Catherine of Aragon?

8. What was the name of King Henry VIII's second wife?

9. What is an annulment?

10. Who was the primary author of the *Book of Common Prayer*?

11. What nickname did Mary Tudor earn due to her persecution of Protestants?

12. What was the effect of Queen Elizabeth I's reign upon the church?

HEARING FROM GOD'S WORD

13. Read 2 Peter 1:19-21. What image does Peter associate with the prophetic Word, the Scriptures?

14. Read 2 Kings 22:1-2. How does this passage describe King Josiah? What similarities are there between King Josiah of Judah and King Edward VI of England?

PRAYER

Now, take time to seek the Lord in prayer, giving thanks to Him, and asking for His undeserved blessings.

- Give thanks to the Lord for faithful men and women who stood for the truth, even at the cost of their lives.

- Ask the Lord to give you courage to stand for the truth of the gospel, no matter what the cost may be.

- Pray that the Lord Jesus would bring an increasing purity to His church in your nation and state/province, so that the Lord would be glorified in the purity and faithfulness of His bride, the church.

23. The Reformation in Scotland

PERSON MATCHING

1. George Wishart
2. David Beaton
3. Mary of Guise
4. Marjory Bowes
5. Mary, Queen of Scots
6. John Knox
7. James VI
8. Thomas Cranmer

a. John Knox's wife
b. Regent over Scotland for a time
c. Queen of Scotland after her mother's regency
d. Burned to death by the Roman Catholic cardinal in Scotland
e. Son of Mary, Queen of Scots
f. Authored the *Book of Common Prayer*
g. Roman Catholic cardinal in Scotland
h. Served as a slave on French galleys

SHORT ANSWER

9. Who wrote The *History of the Reformation in Scotland*?

10. Who did John Knox act as bodyguard for?

11. In what castle was Knox confined for a time, where he was also ordained?

12. Where did Knox minister as a pastor in northern England for a time?

13. What was Knox's opinion of Geneva?

14. What important confession of faith was produced in 1560?

HEARING FROM GOD'S WORD

15. Read 2 Timothy 2:2-4. What does Paul liken the work of ministry to when he writes to Timothy? How did John Knox exemplify this same understanding of ministry?

16. Read 1 Kings 22:14. How did Knox follow in the footsteps of the prophet Micaiah in his interviews with Queen Mary?

PRAYER

Now, take time to pray to the Lord, giving thanks to Him.

- Praise God for the powerful working of the Holy Spirit who gives courage to Christ's people.

- Give thanks to the Lord for the growth of Christ's church in Scotland during the Reformation period.

- Ask the Lord to raise up more preachers like John Knox who trumpet God's Word with authority and who do not fear men.

24. The Catholic Counter-Reformation

TIMELINE MATCHING

1. The Colloquy of Regensburg
2. Founding of the Jesuit order
3. Pope Paul IV issues a list of prohibited books
4. The Council of Trent
5. The St. Bartholomew's Day Massacre
6. The publication of the Reina-Valera Bible
7. Cyril Lucaris becomes Patriarch of Constantinople
8. The Synod of Jerusalem condemns Protestant teaching

a. 1540
b. 1545-1563
c. 1572
d. 1620
e. 1541
f. 1672
g. 1559
h. 1602

SHORT ANSWER

9. List some of the reformers present at the Colloquy of Regensburg.

10. Who founded the Society of Jesus (Jesuits)?

11. Who was one of the most traveled Roman Catholic missionaries of all time, who was a Jesuit?

12. What major Roman Catholic church council condemned Protestant teaching?

13. Name two influential teachers that the Jesuits looked to in their theology and practice?

14. Which French king was responsible for driving the Huguenots out of France?

HEARING FROM GOD'S WORD

15. Read Galatians 1:6-8. What strong warning does Paul give in this passage? How did the Roman Catholics use similar language in their church councils against the true gospel?

PRAYER

Now, take time to pray to the Lord, giving thanks, and seeking His undeserved blessings.

- Thank the Lord for preserving the saving gospel of Jesus Christ in its purity throughout history, and despite the attacks of Satan and false teachers.

- Pray that the Roman Catholic Church as a whole would repent of its rejection of the gospel of God's grace.

- Pray for any Roman Catholics you know personally, asking that the Lord would give them a right understanding of the gospel.

- Ask the Lord to guard you against shifting from the gospel into any false teaching or practice that would harm your soul.

Unit 4 Exam: The Reformation

Total: 40 Points

TIMELINE MATCHING

1. Luther posts the 95 Theses   a. 1521

2. Tyndale's first edition of the English New Testament   b. 1572

3. The English Authorised Version is published   c. 1527

4. The St. Bartholomew's Day Massacre   d. 1517

5. Luther at the Diet of Worms   e. 1492

6. Felix Manz executed   f. 1526

7. Tyndale is executed   g. 1553

8. The publication of the Reina-Valera Bible   h. 1611

9. Death of Edward VI   i. 1536

10. Christopher Columbus discovers the Americas   j. 1602

PERSON MATCHING

11. Desiderius Erasmus

12. Martin Bucer

13. David Beaton

14. Konrad Grebel

15. Heinrich Bullinger

16. George Wishart

17. William Farel

18. Michael Servetus

19. Thomas Cranmer

20. Anna Reinhart

a. Reformer in Strasbourg and mentor to John Calvin

b. One of the founders of the Anabaptist movement

c. Burned to death by the Roman Catholic Cardinal in Scotland

d. Published an edition of the Greek New Testament in 1516

e. Reformer who urged Calvin to come and minister in Geneva

f. Authored the *Book of Common Prayer*

g. Roman Catholic cardinal in Scotland

h. Ulrich Zwingli's wife

i. Zwingli's successor in Zurich

j. Medical doctor who espoused heresy

MULTIPLE CHOICE

21. Which of these men were responsible for reviving the study of Hebrew around the time of the Reformation?

    A. Desiderius Erasmus
    B. Johannes Reuchlin
    C. William Tyndale
    D. John Wycliffe

22. Luther was a member of which monastic order?

    A. The Dominicans
    B. The Franciscans
    C. The Carthusians
    D. The Augustinians

23. Which of these was condemned as a heretic at the Council of Constance?

    A. Martin Luther
    B. William Tyndale
    C. John Huss
    D. John Knox

24. What was eaten in Zurich in the Spring of 1522 at a house gathering, which was forbidden during Lent?

    A. Apples
    B. Steak
    C. Broccoli
    D. Sausage

25. Where did Luther and Zwingli meet to discuss the Lord's Supper, among other doctrinal matters?

    A. Marburg
    B. Wittenberg
    C. Worms
    D. Schleitheim

26. Which of these documents was produced by the Anabaptists?

    A. *67 Articles*
    B. *Book of Concord*
    C. *Schleitheim Confession*
    D. *39 Articles*

27. Which of these documents serves as a confession of faith for the Church of England?

    A. *Scottish Confession*
    B. *39 Articles*
    C. *67 Articles*
    D. *Augsburg Confession*

28. Which French King was addressed in Calvin's *Institutes of the Christian Religion*?

    A. Louis XIV
    B. Francis I
    C. Charles IX
    D. Henry II

29. To what country did the majority of missionaries from Geneva go?

    A. France
    B. England
    C. Spain
    D. Russia

30. Who was the author of *Acts and Monuments of These Latter and Perilous Days*?

    A. Hugh Latimer
    B. Nicholas Ridley
    C. John Foxe
    D. John Walsh

31. In what town did Tyndale complete and publish his first edition of the English New Testament?

    A. Cologne
    B. Worms
    C. Wittenberg
    D. Brussels

32. Who was the second wife of Henry VIII?

    A. Anne Boleyn
    B. Catherine of Aragon
    C. Jane Seymour
    D. Catherine Parr

33. Which of these men preached indulgences?

    A. Albert of Mainz
    B. Johann Tetzel
    C. Johann von Staupitz
    D. Johann Eck

34. Which of these men had a role in forming the most common Spanish translation of the Bible?

    A. Ignatius Loyola
    B. Cyril Lucaris
    C. Cassiodoro de Reina
    D. Gasparo Contarini

35. Which of these figures visited Japan as a Roman Catholic missionary?

    A. Francis Xavier
    B. Ignatius Loyola
    C. Ludolph of Saxony
    D. Johann Gropper

36. Who falsely prophesied Christ's return?

    A. Jans Beukels
    B. Menno Simons
    C. Konrad Grebel
    D. Melchior Hoffman

37. What was the name of Martin Luther's wife?

    A. Anna
    B. Katherine
    C. Idelette
    D. Jane

38. Who wrote the hymn *A Mighty Fortress is Our God*?

    A. John Calvin
    B. Philip Melanchthon
    C. Martin Luther
    D. William Tyndale

39. Which of these groups does NOT practice infant baptism?

    A. Lutherans
    B. Anabaptists
    C. Reformed
    D. Anglicans

40. Where did Ulrich Zwingli die in battle?

    A. Kappel
    B. Constance
    C. Geneva
    D. Zurich

Unit 4 Essay: The Reformation

Write an essay of at least 300 words on a person or topic covered in this unit. Student may choose from the topic suggestions below. However, the student may also choose another topic with the permission of their parent/teacher.

- Using online or book resources, read Luther's *95 Theses*. Then, write an essay explaining the importance and teaching of the *95 Theses*. Quote a few of the *Theses* in your essay.

- Choose one person covered in this unity and write a summary of their life. At the end of your essay, include a few lessons from their life that are edifying for Christians today.

- Using online or book resources, research one of the towns/cities covered in this unit. Explain what the culture, government, and religious life of that town is today compared with the Reformation period.

- Look through the chapters in this unit and choose a quoted Scripture passage. Based on that Scripture passage, write an essay explaining the meaning of the Bible passage. Summarize a few important applications from the passage.

Unit 4 Optional Enrichment Projects

Choose one of these optional enrichment projects to complete Unit 4:

- **Presentation:** Create a 5-minute presentation on a person or event covered in this unit and present to your family or friends. Follow these steps:
    a. Introduce yourself and the subject you will talk about.
    b. Share some interesting facts you learned.
    c. End by stating your summary or opinion based on the facts of the topic.
    d. Thank your audience and invite them to ask any questions.

- **Geography:** Create a list of locations mentioned in this unit. Using online resources, create a map of a particular region (Mediterranean World, or a sublocation such as Italy) and mark key persons and locations in this unit. Use your creativity and artistic skill to produce a map/poster board that is visually pleasing.

- **Timeline:** Using the timeline in the textbook and dates mentioned in the workbook, create your own timeline with poster board. Using internet resources, print pictures of key figures or locations and paste them onto your timeline.

- **Food:** Select a country or region mentioned in this unit. Research the most popular dishes from that particular country or region. Purchase the ingredients necessary and follow the recipe available in the cookbook or online resource and feed your family or friends!

- **Art:** Create a sketch of one of the persons covered in this unit. Or, create a sketch of a major event covered in this unit.

- **Music:** Find and learn a new hymn! Using a book hymnal available to you, or online sources (such as hymnary.org), search for a hymn that was written by one of the people covered in this unit (search for some of the key names covered in this unit), or a hymn written in this period of church history. Learn how to sing the hymn with the family and explore its meaning together. If able, play the melody of the hymn on a musical instrument you have learned.

- **Reading:** Write a book review on a book written by one of the Christians covered in this unit. If the student chooses this essay assignment, it is recommended that the parent/teacher give the student an additional 3-4 weeks to complete the book review. In your essay, explain how this book is still an important resource for Christians. The student is not limited to these ideas, but here are a few short books to get started:

    - *A Little Book on the Christian Life* – John Calvin
    - *The Freedom of the Christian* – Martin Luther
    - *The History of the Reformation* – John Knox
    - *Foxe's Book of Martyrs* – John Foxe

25. Puritans, Separatists, and Covenanters

PERSON MATCHING

1. John Whitgift
2. William Perkins
3. William Laud
4. Oliver Cromwell
5. John Bunyan
6. Margaret Wilson
7. James II
8. Charles II

a. Archbishop of Canterbury during the reign of Charles I, who persecuted the Puritans

b. Wrote *The Pilgrim's Progress*

c. A martyr among the Covenanters

d. Oversaw the Star Chamber

e. Attempted to return England and Scotland to Roman Catholicism

f. Often considered the "father of Puritanism"

g. The monarchy was restored under him

h. Served as Lord Protector over the Commonwealth of England, Scotland, and Ireland

SHORT ANSWER

9. What three forms of church government are listed in this chapter?

10. What were those Christians who separated and worshiped independently of the Church of England known as?

11. At what conference was the production of the English King James Version authorized?

12. Who threw a stool at the Dean of Edinburgh?

13. What assembly of theologians was brought together by the English Parliament and met from 1643 to 1648?

14. What calamity occurred in London in 1666?

HEARING FROM GOD'S WORD

15. Read Ephesians 5:25-27. What is Christ's goal in loving and giving himself for the church? What is the Lord going to bring about through His redemption of the church?

16. Read 2 Corinthians 6:16-18 and 2 Corinthians 7:1. What are the promises described in this passage? What command is given in light of this promise?

PRAYER

Now, take time to pray to our Holy God, asking for His sanctifying work to be completed in you and in the church of Christ as a whole.

- Praise God for His perfect holiness.

- Ask the Lord Jesus to purify His church so that it will be without blemish in teaching and practice.

- Pray that the Lord would purify you for His service, so that you would be a holy vessel, ready for every good work.

26. Pietists, Arminians, and Baptists

TIMELINE MATCHING

1. The Peace of Augsburg   a. 1705

2. *Pia Desideria* published   b. 1722

3. Pietist school established in Halle   c. 1675

4. Moravians establish Herrnhut with Count von Zinzendorf   d. 1732

5. The 100-year prayer meeting begins in Herrnhut   e. 1555

6. First Moravian missionaries set out for St. Thomas   f. 1733

7. Moravian mission to Greenland launched   g. 1618-1619

8. Synod of Dort   h. 1727

SHORT ANSWER

9. Which Swedish King defended Protestantism during the Thirty Years War?

10. What is the collection of Lutheran confessions and catechisms called?

11. Who is considered by most the founder of Pietism?

12. What is a conventicle?

13. What does Herrnhut mean?

14. Whose ideas produced controversy in the Netherlands leading to the Synod of Dort?

15. What well-known Baptist pastor resisted the Downgrade in England?

HEARING FROM GOD'S WORD

16. Read Hebrews 10:23-25. What are Christians to encourage one another toward doing? Why is it important that Christians regularly assemble together? What are some benefits you have received from being in fellowship with other Christians?

PRAYER

Now, take time to pray to our Father in Heaven.

- Give thanks for the blessings of Christian fellowship.

- Ask the Lord to grow you in being an edifying, contributing member in the body of Christ. Ask the Lord to show you opportunities to edify your brothers and sisters in Christ.

- Pray for the unity of your local church, asking that the Lord would enable you to walk in humility, and to maintain the unity of Christ's church.

27. Christianity in Colonial America

PERSON MATCHING

1. Christopher Columbus
2. Leif Erickson
3. James Oglethorpe
4. William Bradford
5. John Eliot
6. Roger Williams
7. William Penn
8. John Witherspoon

a. Landed in Greenland and Canada around AD 1000
b. First missionary to native American tribes
c. Discovered America in AD 1492
d. Founder of the colony of Rhode Island
e. Founder of the colony of Pennsylvania
f. Founder of the colony of Georgia
g. President of the College of New Jersey
h. Wrote the first account of Plymouth Colony

SHORT ANSWER

9. What was the first permanent English settlement in North America?

10. What ship brought the Pilgrim Separatists to Plymouth?

11. How did the *New England Primer* begin with its teaching of the alphabet?

12. What was unique about the colony of Maryland when it was founded?

13. In what colony did the Quakers find refuge?

HEARING FROM GOD'S WORD

14. Read Psalm 33:16-18. What are some of the false hopes listed in these verses? Who is our solid hope? What are some things in the modern day that people hope in for their security?

PRAYER

Now, take time to pray to the Almighty Lord.

- Give thanks to God for the Christian heritage of the United States and how that heritage has affected other parts of the world.

- Thank the Lord for showing mercy to the United States, and to other countries around the world where the Lord has been feared and loved.

- Pray for the United States (or the nation you live in) that its political leaders would honor Jesus Christ as King of kings, and that the laws of the land would be righteous laws, in accord with God's Word.

- Also, pray for local political leadership at the state/province level.

28. The Great Awakening

TIMELINE MATCHING

1. George Whitefield preaches in the open air for the first time in Kingswood
2. George Whitefield departs to be with Christ
3. Jonathan Edwards preaches *Sinners in the Hands of an Angry God* in Enfield, CT
4. John and Charles Wesley record conversion experiences

a. 1770
b. 1741
c. 1738
d. 1739

PERSON MATCHING

5. Benjamin Franklin
6. Charles Wesley
7. George Whitefield
8. John Wesley
9. William Wilberforce

a. Wrote "Hark the Herald Angels Sing"
b. Was called "Dr. Squintum" by some
c. A Christian member of Parliament in England
d. Early American inventor and political leader
e. Embraced Arminian theology in opposition to Whitefield

SHORT ANSWER

10. Approximately how many hymns did Charles Wesley write?

11. Who produced the hymnbook *Olney Hymns*?

12. How does J.I. Packer define revival as quoted in this chapter?

HEARING FROM GOD'S WORD

13. Read Psalm 85:4-7. When God revives His people, what is the effect?

PRAYER

Now, take time to pray to the God of all grace, asking Him to bless the church of Christ all over the world.

- Praise God for how He showed His power in past times through spiritual revivals.

- Ask the Lord to bring times of refreshing to the church in your part of the world.

- Ask the Lord to raise up faithful preachers who would proclaim the gospel with zeal and love.

29. Apostasy and Doctrinal Decline in the Church

PERSON MATCHING

1. Fausto Sozzini

2. John Locke

3. Charles Chauncy

4. Johann Gottfried Eichorn

5. Karl Marx

6. Julius Wellhausen

7. Charles Darwin

8. Charles Hodge

a. German academic who denied the supernatural events in the Old Testament

b. Claimed that Moses did not write the first Five Books of the Bible

c. A Latitudinarian who wanted to allow for Deism, Unitarianism, and Quakers

d. Prominent anti-Trinitarian who used human reason to establish doctrine

e. Wrote *On the Origin of Species*

f. A theologian who wrote against Darwinism

g. Founder of Communist ideology

h. Unitarian pastor of the First Church in Boston

SHORT ANSWER

9. What do Unitarians believe?

10. What do Deists believe?

11. What is the documentary hypothesis?

HEARING FROM GOD'S WORD

12. Read Proverbs 30:5-6. What does this passage say about God's Word? What will happen if we add to God's Word our own ideas?

PRAYER

Now, take time to pray to the Lord, the Creator of Heaven and Earth.

- Thank God for the inspiration, the accuracy, and the relevance of the Bible, which is God's Word.

- Ask God to give you a humble heart to always receive His Word, and not to live by your own ideas.

- Pray that the Lord's truth would be kept pure by the churches in your country. Pray that those churches would humbly submit to the Lord's word, and not add to or take away from the Word of God.

Unit 5 Exam: The Post-Reformation Period

Total: 40 Points

TIMELINE MATCHING

1. The Synod of Dort   a. 1741

2. George Whitefield preaches in the open air for the first time in Kingswood   b. 1517

3. Jonathan Edwards preaches *Sinners in the Hands of an Angry God* in Enfield, CT   c. 1611

4. Luther posts the 95 Theses   d. 1309-1377

5. The English Authorised Version is published   e. 325

6. The Babylonian Captivity of the Papacy (the Avignon Papacy)   f. 1618-1619

7. The Council of Nicaea   g. 570

8. Muhammad born   h. 1732

9. Alopen visits China   i. 1739

10. First Moravian missionaries set out for St. Thomas   j. 635

PERSON MATCHING

11. Christopher Columbus

12. Charles Chauncy

13. Roger Williams

14. Charles Darwin

15. George Whitefield

16. Benjamin Franklin

17. James Oglethorpe

18. David Beaton

19. Heinrich Bullinger

20. John Wycliffe

a. Founder of the colony of Rhode Island

b. Early American inventor and political leader

c. Unitarian pastor of the First Church in Boston

d. Was called "Dr. Squintum" by some

e. Discovered America in AD 1492

f. Roman Catholic cardinal in Scotland

g. Wrote *On the Origin of Species*

h. Reformer who taught at Oxford University

i. Founder of the colony of Georgia

j. Zwingli's successor in Zurich

MULTIPLE CHOICE

21. Which of these confessional documents was produced by the Church of England?

    A. *39 Articles*
    B. *Schleitheim Confession*
    C. *67 Articles*
    D. *Scottish Confession*

22. What form of church government has the three offices of bishop, priest, and deacon?

    A. Congregational
    B. Presbyterian
    C. Episcopal
    D. Independent

23. Who authorized the production of the English *Authorised Version*?

    A. Henry VIII
    B. Edward VI
    C. Elizabeth I
    D. James I

24. Who wrote *The Pilgrim's Progress*?

    A. William Perkins
    B. John Bunyan
    C. Oliver Cromwell
    D. William Ames

25. Who founded a Pietist school in Halle?

    A. Philip Jakob Spener
    B. Count von Zinzendorf
    C. August Hermann Francke
    D. John Wesley

26. Where did the first Moravian missionaries from Herrnhut go?

    A. Greenland
    B. St. Thomas
    C. Brazil
    D. Canada

27. How many Articles of Remonstrance did the Arminians argue for at the Synod of Dort?

    A. Three
    B. Ten
    C. Four
    D. Five

28. Who pastored the Metropolitan Tabernacle in London?

    A. Charles Spurgeon
    B. A.W. Pink
    C. Daniel Parker
    D. Benjamin Keach

29. In what modern-day state is Plymouth Plantation located?

    A. Rhode Island
    B. Massachusetts
    C. New York
    D. Connecticut

30. This man had a significant spiritual experience at Aldersgate Street, London.

    A. Charles Wesley
    B. George Whitefield
    C. John Wesley
    D. Jonathan Edwards

31. Who wrote the hymn *Amazing Grace*?

    A. John Newton
    B. John Owen
    C. William Cowper
    D. John Bunyan

32. Which of these men defended biblical truth?

    A. Julius Wellhausen
    B. Karl Marx
    C. Johann Gottfried Eichorn
    D. J. Gresham Machen

33. Where did Luther and Zwingli meet to discuss the Lord's Supper, among other doctrinal matters?

    A. Marburg
    B. Wittenberg
    C. Worms
    D. Schleitheim

34. Who taught that man is NOT born corrupt in sin?

    A. Pelagius
    B. Augustine
    C. Arius
    D. Nestorius

35. In what place did the Waldensian movement originate?

    A. London
    B. Lyons
    C. Paris
    D. Rome

36. Who was the author of *Acts and Monuments of These Latter and Perilous Days*?

    A. Hugh Latimer
    B. Nicholas Ridley
    C. John Foxe
    D. John Walsh

37. According to tradition, which apostle first took the Gospel to India?

    A. John
    B. Peter
    C. Mark
    D. Thomas

38. Served as Bishop of Hippo

    A. Tertullian
    B. Origen
    C. Augustine
    D. Irenaeus

39. Which of these was condemned as a heretic at the Council of Constance?

    A. Martin Luther
    B. William Tyndale
    C. John Huss
    D. John Knox

40. Whose philosophy did Thomas Aquinas revive and integrate into his theology?

    A. Socrates
    B. Plato
    C. Demosthenes
    D. Aristotle

Unit 5 Essay:
The Post-Reformation Period

Write an essay of at least 300 words on a person or topic covered in this unit. Student may choose from the topic suggestions below. However, the student may also choose another topic with the permission of their parent/teacher.

- Choose one state in the USA and write an essay detailing its religious history. Use the textbook of this course, or other book resources available. Additional history books on that particular state may be procured from a local library.

- Choose one person covered in this unity and write a summary of their life. At the end of your essay, include a few lessons from their life that are edifying for Christians today.

- Using online or book resources, research one of the towns/cities covered in this unit. Explain what the culture, government, and religious life of that town is today compared with the period of time covered in this unit.

- Look through the chapters in this unit and choose a quoted Scripture passage. Based on that Scripture passage, write an essay explaining the meaning of the Bible passage. Summarize a few important applications from the passage.

- Write an essay summarizing significant events during the Great Awakening.

Unit 5 Optional Enrichment Projects

Choose one of these optional enrichment projects to complete Unit 5:

- **Presentation:** Create a 5-minute presentation on a person or event covered in this unit and present to your family or friends. Follow these steps:
    a. a. Introduce yourself and the subject you will talk about.
    b. b. Share some interesting facts you learned.
    c. c. End by stating your summary or opinion based on the facts of the topic.
    d. d. Thank your audience and invite them to ask any questions.

- **Geography:** Create a list of locations mentioned in this unit. Using online resources, create a map of a particular region (for example, Europe, America, or a particular state or province) and mark key persons and locations in this unit. Use your creativity and artistic skill to produce a map/poster board that is visually pleasing.

- **Timeline:** Using the timeline in the textbook and dates mentioned in the workbook, create your own timeline with poster board. Using internet resources, print pictures of key figures or locations and paste them onto your timeline.

- **Food:** Select a country or region mentioned in this unit. Research the most popular dishes from that particular country or region. Purchase the ingredients necessary and follow the recipe available in the cookbook or online resource and feed your family or friends!

- **Art:** Create a sketch of one of the persons covered in this unit. Or, create a sketch of a major event covered in this unit.

- **Music:** Find and learn a new hymn! Using a book hymnal available to you, or online sources (such as hymnary.org), search for a hymn that was written by one of the people covered in this unit (search for some of the key names covered in this unit), or a hymn written in this period of church history. Learn how to sing the hymn with the family and explore its meaning together. If able, play the melody of the hymn on a musical instrument you have learned.

- **Bible:** Find a sermon preached/written by one of the pastors/preachers covered in this unit. Read it out-loud with your family during family worship time, either in portions, or all at once depending on length. Discuss applications from the message and pray afterward.

- **Reading:** Write a book review on a book written by one of the Christians covered in this unit. If the student chooses this essay assignment, it is recommended that the parent/teacher give the student an additional 3-4 weeks to complete the book review. In your essay, explain how this book is still an important resource for Christians. The student is not limited to these ideas, but here are a few to get started:

    - *The Pilgrim's Progress* – John Bunyan
    - *The Mortification of Sin* – John Owen
    - *The Life of God in the Soul of Man* – Henry Scougal
    - *An Alarm to the Unconverted* – Joseph Alleine
    - *A Practical View of Christianity* – William Wilberforce
    - *Grace Abounding to the Chief of Sinners* – John Bunyan

30. The Modern Missionary Movement

PERSON MATCHING

1. William Carey
2. Henry Martyn
3. Adoniram Judson
4. John G. Paton
5. Samuel Ajayi Crowther
6. Andrew Bonar
7. Alfred Edersheim
8. Sarah Boardman

a. Translated the Bible into Burmese
b. Kidnapped slave who became the first African Anglican bishop
c. English cobbler who became a missionary to India
d. Jewish convert to Christianity who wrote *The Life and Times of Jesus the Messiah*
e. Adoniram Judson's second wife
f. Translated the New Testament into Persian
g. Missionary to the New Hebrides
h. Scottish missionary to Israel

SHORT ANSWER

9. What century is often called the "greatest century of missions?"

10. How many years did William Carey labor in India before a conversion occurred?

11. What was the practice of *Sati*?

12. What conflict led to Adoniram Judson being imprisoned?

13. What island of the New Hebrides did John Paton first minister on?

HEARING FROM GOD'S WORD

14. Read Psalm 22:27-28. What prophetic promise is contained in these verses? How should this passage shape how we think about Christian missions?

PRAYER

Now, take time to pray to the Lord, the Maker of heaven and earth.

- Praise the Lord Jesus Christ for His reign over all things, and how His gospel has gone all over the world, saving the peoples of the earth.
- Acknowledge Jesus to be King over all, and pray that His reign would be acknowledged by all the nations of the earth.

- Pray that God's kingdom would come in the earth, by the defeat of Satan, by the ingathering of God's people, and ultimately with the return of Jesus Christ.

- Ask God to advance the reign of His grace in your heart, in your family, and in your church.

31. Revivals and Cults in the 19th Century

TIMELINE MATCHING

1. The year James McGready arrived in Kentucky
2. Joseph Smith creates the *Book of Mormon*
3. The "Great Disappointment"
4. The Welsh Revival
5. Revival meetings in Cane Ridge, Kentucky
6. Fox sisters conduct séances
7. "Killing Times" in Scotland
8. Thomas Chalmers suffers the loss of his sister and uncle

a. 1827
b. 1859
c. 1801
d. 1796
e. 1808
f. 1844
g. 1848
h. 1660-1688

SHORT ANSWER

9. What preacher confronted Charles Finney in New Lebanon in 1827?

10. Who was responsible for the idea of the "Anxious Bench"?

11. Name the two founders of the Restoration Movement.

12. Who founded the Jehovah's Witnesses cult?

13. What cult did Joseph Smith form?

14. In what town did the Welsh Revival begin?

HEARING FROM GOD'S WORD

15. Read 1 John 4:1. What warning does this verse provide?

16. Read Luke 11:13. What promise does our Lord Jesus make in this verse?

PRAYER

Now, take time to pray to our Father in heaven.

- Ask the Lord for growing discernment so that you will not be deceived by false teaching. Pray that God will grow you in a mature understanding of His Holy Word.

- Pray that the plans of Satan, using false teaching, would be defeated by the faithful preaching of God's Word.

- Ask the Lord for times of spiritual refreshing in your local church, and in all the churches in your local area.

32. Fundamentalists and Liberals

PERSON MATCHING

1. Woodrow Wilson
2. J. Gresham Machen
3. Harry Emerson Fosdick
4. Pearl S. Buck
5. Adolf von Harnack
6. Joseph Smith
7. Charles Taze Russell
8. Asahel Nettleton

a. Preached "Shall the Fundamentalists Win?"
b. A woman missionary who rejected orthodox Bible-based teachings
c. Wrote *Christianity and Liberalism*
d. German theologian who propagated liberal theology
e. Founder of the Jehovah's Witnesses cult
f. Preacher during the Second Great Awakening
g. 28th President of the United States
h. Founder of the Mormon cult

SHORT ANSWER

9. How did H. Richard Niebuhr summarize liberal theology as quoted in this chapter?

10. What important book was published in 1910?

11. What institution did J. Gresham Machen found in 1929?

12. What denomination did Machen help in founding?

HEARING FROM GOD'S WORD

13. Read 1 Corinthians 15:3-5. In this passage, Paul summarizes those doctrines of "first importance." What are the core and essential beliefs of Christianity summarized in these verses?

14. Read 1 Corinthians 15:12-15. What would be the consequence if the resurrection of Christ was not true?

PRAYER

Now, take time to pray to the God of all truth.

- Praise God for the clarity of the Bible, which reveals truth to us, and which enables us to discern between true and false.

- Praise the Lord Jesus for preserving His true church against dangerous error that would harm souls.

- Pray for purity of doctrine, worship, and practice in your local church. Pray for your local pastor/elders that they would be faithful to guard the deposit of truth that the Lord Jesus entrusted to them.

- Pray for any friends or family members who have been affected by cults or false teaching, that God would grant them a true knowledge of the gospel.

33. Persecutions in Eastern Europe

TIMELINE MATCHING

1. The Bolshevik Revolution   a. 1960

2. First Lutheran church established in Russia   b. 1948

3. Brother Andrew visits Moscow   c. 1917

4. Richard Wurmbrand arrested   d. 1989

5. Richard Wurmbrand founds the Voice of the Martyrs   e. 1991

6. Berlin Wall torn down   f. 1576

7. The Soviet Union collapses   g. 1967

8. Vladimir Lenin dies   h. 1924

SHORT ANSWER

9. What was the largest church in Russia at the time of the Bolshevik Revolution?

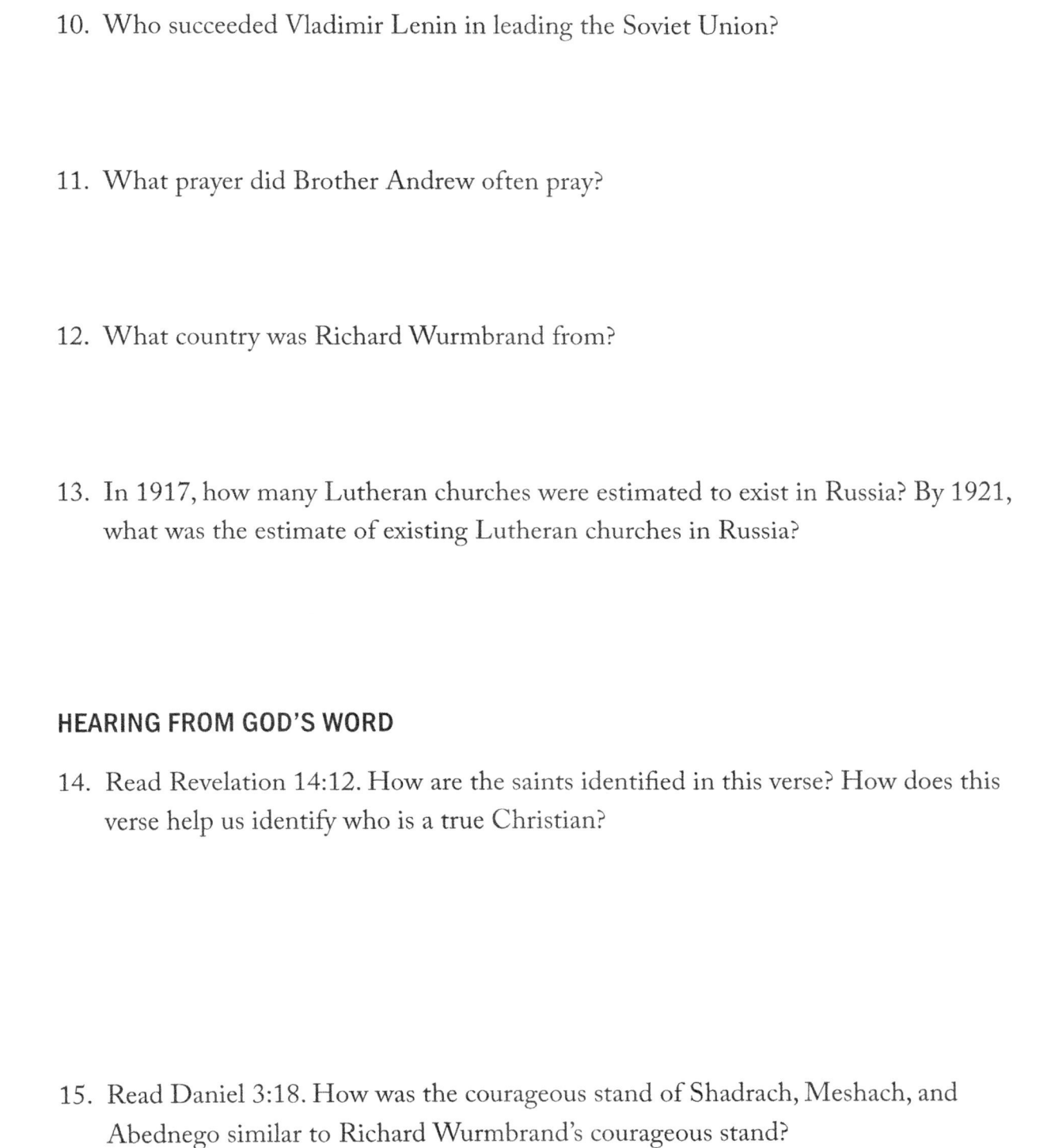

10. Who succeeded Vladimir Lenin in leading the Soviet Union?

11. What prayer did Brother Andrew often pray?

12. What country was Richard Wurmbrand from?

13. In 1917, how many Lutheran churches were estimated to exist in Russia? By 1921, what was the estimate of existing Lutheran churches in Russia?

HEARING FROM GOD'S WORD

14. Read Revelation 14:12. How are the saints identified in this verse? How does this verse help us identify who is a true Christian?

15. Read Daniel 3:18. How was the courageous stand of Shadrach, Meshach, and Abednego similar to Richard Wurmbrand's courageous stand?

PRAYER

Now, take time to pray to our merciful Father in heaven.

- Praise God for giving His servants faith and courage to stand against evil in times of persecution.

- Give thanks to God for the defeat of communism in certain parts of the world. Pray for the defeat of communism in other parts of the world (such as Cuba or China)

- Ask the Lord to strengthen the church in your nation to be courageous against evil. Ask God to enable the church in your land to be a faithful witness for the Lord Jesus Christ.

34. Christians in World War II

PERSON MATCHING

1. Adolf Hitler
2. Dietrich Bonhoeffer
3. Corrie ten Boom
4. Henry Gerecke
5. Sixtus O'Connor
6. Herman Goering
7. Wilhelm Keitel
8. Fritz Sauckel

a. German Christian who was executed by the Nazis in 1945

b. US Army Lutheran chaplain who ministered during the Nuremberg Trials

c. Leader of the Nazis in World War II

d. Commander of the German Luftwaffe during World War II

e. Hid Jews in her home in the Netherlands

f. US Army Roman Catholic chaplain who ministered during the Nuremberg Trials

g. German labor minister who served in Hitler's administration

h. Commander of the German Army during World War II

SHORT ANSWER

9. What happened on September 1, 1939?

10. Approximately how many people died in World War II?

11. What important book did Corrie ten Boom write?

12. Where did the international tribunal against the Nazis occur?

13. Which former German Nazi leader demanded to partake of the Lord's Supper but was refused because of his unbelief?

HEARING FROM GOD'S WORD

14. Read Romans 12:21. How do the stories of Dietrich Bonhoeffer, Corrie ten Boom, and Henry Gerecke illustration the truth of this verse? Explain how each of these Christians sought to do good.

PRAYER

Now, take time to pray to the Lord Almighty.

- Praise God for sustaining His people through war, famine, and other tribulations, and giving them the faith to endure, as we learned in this chapter.

- Give thanks to God that none of these things can separate us from God's love (Rom. 8:38-39).

- Ask God to enable you to face evil not by doing evil in return, but instead by doing good. Ask the Lord for the grace to love your enemies, to do good to those who oppose you.

35. Persecutions in China and Korea

TIMELINE AND LOCATION REVIEW

1. The Boxer Rebellion took place in _____.

2. The Three-Self Church was established in AD _____.

3. The Korean Pentecost took place in AD _____.

4. The Korean War lasted from AD _____ to AD _____.

5. Emperor Cixi decreed that all foreigners should be killed in AD _____.

SHORT ANSWER

6. In what region was the Boxer Rebellion particularly fierce against Christians?

7. What is the name of China's first communist leader?

8. Who received a copy of the Bible in China after praying that God would give him a copy?

9. Which two Presbyterian missionaries were witnesses of the Korean revival?

HEARING FROM GOD'S WORD

10. Read Ephesians 6:12-13. When people oppose us and our faith, what does this passage help us to remember?

PRAYER

Now, take time to pray to the God of infinite power.

- Pray for persecuted brothers and sisters in Christ in other parts of the world (ideas include China, North Korea, Afghanistan, Nigeria, Pakistan, etc.) asking that the Lord would strengthen them to endure suffering and to stand fast for Jesus Christ.

- Praise the Lord for His power shown in the lives of His saints, who were able to endure extreme suffering for the sake of His name.

36. Christian Leaders and Movements of the 20th Century

PERSON MATCHING

1. C.S. Lewis
2. D. Martyn Lloyd-Jones
3. Billy Graham
4. Elisabeth Elliott
5. William J. Seymour
6. Jay Adams
7. Henry Morris
8. Ken Ham

a. Preacher at Westminster Chapel

b. Lost her husband to the Waorani natives of Ecuador

c. An Oxford scholar who wrote *Mere Christianity*

d. Founder of the "nouthetic counseling" or biblical counseling movement

e. American evangelist who preached all over the world

f. Preacher at the Azusa Street mission

g. Founder of Answers in Genesis

h. One of the authors of *The Genesis Flood*

SHORT ANSWER

9. Before he became a preacher, what did D. Martyn Lloyd-Jones do as a profession?

10. How did Elisabeth Elliot show remarkable courage and love after the death of her husband?

11. Where did the Pentecostal movement begin?

12. What American thinker advocated for education without the fear of God?

13. What movement was born out of the publication of *The Genesis Flood*?

14. In what region of the world is Christianity growing most rapidly at present?

HEARING FROM GOD'S WORD

15. Read Philippians 2:10-11. What will happen one day?

PRAYER

Now, take time to pray to our Father in heaven.

- Thank the Lord for all that you have learned in this survey of Church History.

- Praise the Lord Jesus Christ for His reign over all, and the power of His gospel which has transformed the world.

- Pray, "Come, Lord Jesus" asking that our Lord would return and bring the kingdom to completion.

Unit 6 Exam: The Age of Missions and the Modern Period

Total: 40 Points

TIMELINE MATCHING

1. The "Great Disappointment"   a. 1859

2. The Welsh Revival   b. 1948

3. Joseph Smith creates the *Book of Mormon*   c. 1991

4. The Bolshevik Revolution   d. 1980

5. Richard Wurmbrand arrested   e. 1827

6. The Soviet Union collapses   f. 1907

7. Three-Self Church established in China   g. 1660–1688

8. The Korean Pentecost   h. 1917

9. "Killing Times" in Scotland   i. 1576

10. First Lutheran church established in Russia   j. 1844

PERSON MATCHING

11. J. Gresham Machen

12. Dietrich Bonhoeffer

13. Adolf Hitler

14. Harry Emerson Fosdick

15. Charles Taze Russell

16. Corrie ten Boom

17. Henry Gerecke

18. C.S. Lewis

19. Billy Graham

20. Woodrow Wilson

a. Founder of the Jehovah's Witnesses cult

b. Wrote *Christianity and Liberalism*

c. Leader of the Nazis in World War II

d. Hid Jews in her home in the Netherlands

e. An Oxford scholar who wrote *Mere Christianity*

f. Preached "Shall the Fundamentalists Win?"

g. German Christian who was executed by the Nazis in 1945

h. 28th President of the United States

i. American evangelist who preached all over the world

j. US Army Lutheran chaplain who ministered during the Nuremberg Trials

MULTIPLE CHOICE

21. Which missionary established a college in Serampore?

    A. Henry Martyn
    B. William Carey
    C. Adoniram Judson
    D. Andrew Bonar

22. Which missionary journeyed to Tabriz, Iran to visit the Shah?

    A. William Carey
    B. Robert Murray M'Cheyne
    C. Andrew Bonar
    D. Henry Martyn

23. Who brought the gospel to the cannibals of the New Hebrides?

    A. William Carey
    B. Adoniram Judson
    C. John G. Paton
    D. Henry Martyn

24. Who is generally considered the first evangelist of the Second Great Awakening?

    A. Charles Grandison Finney
    B. Asahel Nettleton
    C. Timothy Dwight
    D. James McGready

25. Which group claims that their holy book was translated from golden plates given by God?

    A. Latter Day Saints (Mormons)
    B. Jehovah's Witnesses
    C. Spiritualists
    D. Adventists

26. Which of these men defended biblical truth?

    A. Adolf von Harnack
    B. Harry Emerson Fosdick
    C. J. Gresham Machen
    D. Albrecht Ritschl

27. Who was the communist leader who led the Bolshevik Revolution?

    A. Adolf Hitler
    B. Vladimir Lenin
    C. Joseph Stalin
    D. Mao Zedong

28. Who smuggled Bibles into the Soviet Union?

    A. Andrew van der Bijl
    B. Richard Wurmbrand
    C. Dietrich Bonhoeffer
    D. Gheorghiu Dej

29. Where was Dietrich Bonhoeffer executed?

    A. Dachau
    B. Auschwitz
    C. Ravensbruck
    D. Flossenburg

30. Which country imposed an evil one-child policy on its citizens?

    A. North Korea
    B. China
    C. Japan
    D. South Korea

31. Where did the Korean revival occur?

    A. Pyongyang
    B. Seoul
    C. Busan
    D. Nampo

32. Which of these documents was produced by the Anabaptists?

    A. *67 Articles*
    B. *Book of Concord*
    C. *Schleitheim Confession*
    D. *39 Articles*

33. The first martyr to die in the Book of Acts

    A. James
    B. Stephen
    C. Peter
    D. John

34. How many Articles of Remonstrance did the Arminians argue for at the Synod of Dort?

    A. Three
    B. Ten
    C. Four
    D. Five

35. Who wrote the hymn *Amazing Grace*?

    A. John Newton
    B. John Owen
    C. William Cowper
    D. John Bunyan

36. What heresy states that human beings are NOT born with a depraved, sinful condition inherited from Adam?

    A. Arianism
    B. Sabellianism
    C. Pelagianism
    D. Eutychianism

37. Who wrote *The Pilgrim's Progress*?

    A. William Perkins
    B. John Bunyan
    C. Oliver Cromwell
    D. William Ames

38. Which of these men had a role in forming the most common Spanish translation of the Bible?

   A. Ignatius Loyola
   B. Cyril Lucaris
   C. Cassiodoro de Reina
   D. Gasparo Contarini

39. Who wrote *An Enquiry into the Obligations of Christians to use Means for the Conversion of the Heathens*?

   A. William Carey
   B. Andrew Bonar
   C. William Gouge
   D. Charles Simeon

40. Which of these men served the church in Nigeria?

   A. Robert Murray M'Cheyne
   B. Samuel Ajayi Crowther
   C. Cotton Mather
   D. George Boardman

Unit 6 Essay: The Age of Missions and the Modern Period

Write an essay of at least 300 words on a person or topic covered in this unit. Student may choose from the topic suggestions below. However, the student may also choose another topic with the permission of their parent/teacher.

- Research the Church of Jesus Christ of Latter Day Saints (LDS) or the Jehovah's Witnesses cults. Write an essay explaining a few of the important doctrinal matters where these groups depart from Scripture. Use Scripture to defend sound doctrine on those points. The student may consult Walter Martin's *The Kingdom of the Cults*, or CARM.org.

- Using an online source such as Voice of the Martyrs or Open Doors, write an essay explaining the situation for Christians in persecuted countries today. Include at least one eyewitness testimony from that country.

- Choose one person from this unit and write a biographical essay on their life and contributions.

Unit 6 Optional Enrichment Projects

Choose one of these optional enrichment projects to complete Unit 6:

- **Presentation:** Create a 5-minute presentation on a person or event covered in this unit and present to your family or friends. Follow these steps:

    a. Introduce yourself and the subject you will talk about.
    b. Share some interesting facts you learned.
    c. End by stating your summary or opinion based on the facts of the topic.
    d. Thank your audience and invite them to ask any questions.

- **Geography:** Create a list of locations mentioned in this unit. Using online resources, create a map of a particular region (Western Europe, Eastern Europe, Africa, etc.) and mark key persons and locations in this unit. Use your creativity and artistic skill to produce a map/poster board that is visually pleasing.

- **Timeline:** Using the timeline in the textbook and dates mentioned in the workbook, create your own timeline with poster board. Using internet resources, print pictures of key figures or locations and paste them onto your timeline.

- **Food:** Select a country or region mentioned in this unit. Research the most popular dishes from that particular country or region. Purchase the ingredients necessary and follow the recipe available in the cookbook or online resource and feed your family or friends!

- **Art:** Create a sketch of one of the persons covered in this unit. Or, create a sketch of a major event covered in this unit.

- **Music:** Find and learn a new hymn! Using a book hymnal available to you, or online sources (such as hymnary.org), search for a hymn that was written by one of the people covered in this unit (search for some of the key names covered in this unit), or a hymn written in this period of church history. Learn how to sing the hymn with the family and explore its meaning together. If able, play the melody of the hymn on a musical instrument you have learned.

- **Bible:** Find a sermon preached/written by one of the pastors/preachers covered in this unit. Read it out-loud with your family during family worship time, either in portions, or all at once depending on length. Discuss applications from the message and pray afterward.

- **Reading:** Write a book review on a book written by one of the Christians covered in this unit. If the student chooses this essay assignment, it is recommended that the parent/teacher give the student an additional 3-4 weeks to complete the book review. In your essay, explain how this book is still an important resource for Christians. The student is not limited to these ideas, but here are a few to get started:

    - *God's Smuggler* – Brother Andrew (also available in a Young Reader's edition)
    - *The Hiding Place* – Corrie ten Boom (also available in a Young Reader's edition)
    - *The Heavenly Man* – Brother Yun
    - *Tortured for Christ* – Richard Wurmbrand
    - *Autobiography* – John G. Paton
    - *Through Gates of Splendor* – Elisabeth Elliot
    - *The Screwtape Letters* – C.S. Lewis
    - *The Pursuit of God* – A.W. Tozer

Answer Key

CHAPTER 1: IN THE FULLNESS OF TIME

1. 54, 68
2. 67
3. Patmos
4. Jerusalem
5. Jerusalem, Judea, Samaria, end
6. Before Christ
7. Anno Domini (in the Year of our Lord)
8. Luke
9. The Great Commission
10. The Holy Spirit came with power upon the disciples, empowering them for their worldwide mission, enabling them to speak in other languages and to preach the gospel.
11. Stephen
12. Approximately 2,800 miles
13. Emperor Nero
14. The Gospel of John, 1 John, 2 John, 3 John, Revelation
15. Athens
16. The foundation of the church is the apostles and prophets. The cornerstone of the church is Jesus Christ.
17. The churches had peace and were edified. They walked in the fear of the Lord, and they experienced the comfort of the Holy Spirit. The churches were multiplying.

CHAPTER 2: THE CHURCH FACES OPPOSITION

1. 64
2. 81, 96
3. 177
4. 312
5. Marcus Aurelius
6. Christians were called atheists because they denied all the false gods of Rome, and only worshiped one God.
7. Tacitus
8. Eusebius
9. *Religio licita* means "lawful religion." *Religio illicita* means "unlawful religion."
10. Diocletian
11. The Apostle John
12. Blandina
13. Constantine
14. *The Martyrdom of Polycarp*
15. Witness
16. Peter says that the effect of trials is to prove the genuineness of our faith. Trials purify and refine our faith much like fire purifies gold. But in the case of our faith, faith purified and refined is far more precious than gold that perishes. Our faith tested brings praise and glory to Jesus Christ.
17. This passage tells us that Christians *must* enter the kingdom of God through *many* tribulations. Every Christian must experience trials in life.

CHAPTER 3: WRITINGS FROM THE EARLY CHURCH

1. c
2. a
3. e
4. b
5. d
6. The Apostolic Fathers
7. The church in Corinth
8. Seven
9. Bishops, elders, and deacons
10. *The Didache*
11. We do not know.
12. The *Didascalia Apostolorum*
13. Eusebius of Caesarea
14. Paul mentions overseers (translated as bishops in the NKJV and KJV) and deacons.
15. Exact list will vary.

CHAPTER 4: CHRISTIAN WORSHIP AND DOCTRINAL DEVELOPMENT

1. c
2. a
3. b
4. g
5. d
6. h
7. e
8. f
9. The first day of the week (the Lord's Day)
10. Summary will vary. Those converts who were to be baptized often went through an extended period

of instruction. This was called "catechesis," a word that means "instruction" or "teaching." Hippolytus writes that this period could last up to three years. Not only were the converts instructed, but their conduct was observed. For those who had practiced various kinds of sinful pagan behaviors, it was important that those ungodly practices would cease before baptism. When the day of baptism came, the disciple was to renounce all the works of the devil and declare their repentance. Some early church documents indicate that the baptismal candidate was sometimes baptized naked (men and women being separated). The bishop or elder presiding would ask the disciple if they believed in the Father, the Son, and the Holy Spirit. Following the baptism, the baptized would be dried off and clothed (sometimes with a white robe). This was to symbolize putting off the old sinful nature and putting on Christ (Eph. 4:22-24; Gal. 3:27). The bishop would then pray over the baptized disciple, for the work of the Holy Spirit. The newly baptized person would partake of the Lord's Supper. In some cases, there was the tradition of giving the baptized milk and honey (signifying their entrance into the "Promised Land").

11. Hippolytus and Cyprian
12. Tertullian
13. The Greek word for fish (icthus) was a code word for "Jesus Christ, Son of God, Savior" in Greek.
14. Christians universally condemned the practice of abortion. Christians also rescued and adopted many children who were left to die.
15. Callistus
16. The Council of Nicaea. AD 325
17. The Council of Chalcedon. AD 451
18. Augustine of Hippo
19. Luke's list includes the disciples continuing to receive and learn more of the apostles' doctrine, participation in fellowship with other Christians, the breaking of bread, and prayer.
20. Unbelievers will find it strange that Christians do not participate in standard Gentile practices. Unbelievers will also mock or speak evil of Christians for being different.

CHAPTER 5: LEADERS OF THE EARLY CHURCH

1. Lyons
2. 215
3. 207
4. 553
5. Alexandria
6. d
7. c
8. f
9. a
10. b
11. e
12. Irenaeus of Lyons
13. Tertullian of Carthage
14. Allegorical and speculative
15. Tertullian said "what has Athens to do with Jerusalem?" He also wrote strongly against Aristotle. He believed that Christian teaching and pagan philosophy were irreconcilable.
16. Tertullian used logic, sarcasm, and humor to defeat false teaching.
17. A Christian disciple in training for baptism.
18. Paul warns against false philosophy that is according to human tradition, and not according to the person and teachings of Jesus Christ. Answers will vary in terms of modern-day application. We should seek to check all teachings against what the Word of God reveals as true. We should be wary of human philosophies that are not rooted in the fear of God, or in the teachings of Jesus Christ. We should make sure that all of our thinking is obedient to Jesus (2 Cor. 10:4-5).
19. By speaking the truth in love to one another, we grow more mature. Every part of Christ's body (that is, every person in the church) contributes to the maturation of the body by edifying speech and acts of love.

CHAPTER 6: MORE LEADERS OF THE EARLY CHURCH

1. d
2. a
3. f
4. g
5. e

6. b
7. h
8. c
9. Athanasius
10. Athanasius' Festal Letter 39
11. Theodosius was responsible for ordering a mass slaughter and he had not yet repented of his sin.
12. Romans 13:14
13. King Alaric
14. Golden-mouthed
15. The Septuagint (Seventy)
16. Basil of Caesarea, Gregory of Nyssa, Gregory of Nazianzus
17. Bethlehem
18. A faithful elder serves with a willing heart, not seeking money, but caring for the spiritual needs of Christ's flock. Faithful elders are not to abuse their authority by domineering behavior. Faithful elders should be examples of godly behavior to Christ's people.
19. The purpose of pastors and teachers is to equip the saints for ministry work, and to build up the church in maturity.

UNIT 1 EXAM: THE EARLY CHURCH
1. b
2. i
3. g
4. a
5. f
6. h
7. c
8. d
9. j
10. e
11. f
12. d
13. h
14. b
15. j
16. a
17. c
18. e
19. g
20. i
21. C
22. C
23. B
24. A
25. D
26. B
27. D
28. C
29. A
30. C
31. B
32. A
33. C
34. D
35. A
36. B
37. A
38. D
39. C
40. B

UNIT 1 ESSAY: THE EARLY CHURCH
Graded by parent/teacher

UNIT 1 OPTIONAL ENRICHMENT PROJECTS
Graded by parent/teacher

CHAPTER 7: MISSIONARY EXPANSION
1. 430
2. 597
3. 563
4. 496
5. 635
6. Petrarch
7. Ulfilas
8. King Alaric
9. Patrick
10. The Venerable Bede
11. Augustine of Canterbury
12. King Clovis
13. Cyril and Methodius
14. Alfred the Great
15. The Apostle Thomas

16. The prophecy speaks of the Gentile nations coming to worship the one true God, and to experience the light of God's glory. As the gospel penetrated into new lands, the promise of God's salvation coming to the nations has been fulfilled. It continues to be fulfilled today as missionaries take the gospel to new lands.
17. The petition in verses 1-2 is a prayer for God's mercy and blessing to be upon God's people, and that God's salvation would be made known among the nations. The promise of verse 7 states that all the ends of the earth will one day fear the Lord.

CHAPTER 8: CHRISTIAN MONASTICISM

1. d
2. a
3. e
4. b
5. f
6. c
7. The practice of severe self-discipline by denying oneself food and water for a time, or denying oneself sleep, and withholding oneself from other various pleasures of life in order to be self-disciplined.
8. Eremetic monastics are those who live alone (solitary). Cenobitic monastics are those monks who live together in community under a common rule.
9. Egypt
10. Nursia
11. The Rule of St. Benedict
12. Worship, manual labor, and study
13. Answers may include: Augustinians, Cluniacs, Cistercians, Franciscans, Dominicans, and Carmelites
14. Abbot
15. Answers will vary. Paul explains in Colossians 2 that imposing numerous man-made regulations as a burden does not really help to stop the indulgence of sinful desires. He also says these regulations may be an expression of false humility rather than true heart religion. He also writes that such rules are the commandments and doctrines of men. In 1 Timothy 4, Paul says it is a sign of apostasy and a doctrine of demons to forbid things God made good such as marriage and various foods.
16. Answers will vary.

CHAPTER 9: THE RISE OF ISLAM

1. 570
2. 622
3. Tours
4. 1095
5. 1291
6. Damascus
7. Allah
8. Mecca
9. Surah 4 of the Qur'an teaches an incorrect understanding of the Trinity. Surah 4 also denies Jesus' death by crucifixion and His Resurrection.
10. Answers:
    - The *Shahadah*, the basic creed of Islam, "There is no God but Allah and Muhammad is his prophet."
    - The *Salah*, prayer five times a day facing Mecca.
    - The *Zakah*, giving to the poor.
    - The *Sawm*, fasting during the holy month of Ramadan.
    - The *Hajj*, the pilgrimage to Mecca to be made at least once in a lifetime.
11. *Deus vult!* (God wills it!)
12. Richard the Lionhearted
13. Raymond Lull
14. John of Damascus
15. Our weapons are not carnal in the sense that they involve physical things like swords, spears, and shields. Rather, the Christian's warfare is to fight in the power of the Spirit against false doctrine, Satanic temptation, and any thinking that is contrary to God's Word. We are to take every thought captive to be obedient to the Lord Jesus Christ.
16. Peter instructs us to defend the faith humbly and in the fear of God, and to set apart God as the Lord in our hearts, humbly submitting to him. This means we should not approach the defense of the faith in a proud manner.

CHAPTER 10: THE DEVELOPMENT OF THE PAPACY

1. f
2. c
3. a
4. d
5. g
6. b
7. e
8. h
9. The word "vicar" means "to stand in the place of." Hence, to be the vicar of Christ is to stand in place of Christ as His earthly representative. To be the vicar of God is to be the direct representative of God on earth.
10. Gregory stated: "Whosoever calls himself universal priest, or desires to be called so, was the forerunner of Antichrist."
11. The document claimed that the Emperor Constantine had granted to Pope Sylvester the Lateran Palace in Rome, and a right to regions in Roman and Italian territory.
12. Benedict IX
13. One goal of the Cluniac Revival was to bring back the discipline and purity of the Rule of St. Benedict.
14. Answers:
    - The Roman pope alone is universal bishop.
    - The pope alone can depose and reinstate bishops.
    - The pope may be judged by no one.
    - The Roman Church has never erred and will never err.
    - The pope may depose emperors.
15. Henry IV humbled himself before Pope Gregory VII (Hildebrand), begging him for mercy after Henry had been excommunicated.
16. Our Lord Jesus set an example of sacrificial service. He gave up His life as a ransom for many. Gentile leadership in the world is characterized by domineering behavior whereby people attempt to become superior over others. But the example of Christ which He set for his under shepherds is servant leadership.
17. Paul contrasts selfish-ambition and conceit (thinking highly of oneself, seeking power and honor) vs. humility which is demonstrated in considering others more significant than ourselves.

CHAPTER 11: SCHISM IN THE CHURCH

1. d
2. c
3. e
4. b
5. f
6. a
7. This word comes from a Greek word appearing in the New Testament that describes divisions or factions. A schism, then, is a tearing apart of something that once was together.
8. The Eastern and Western branches of the church separated.
9. Exact list will vary. Answers may include:
    - The Western church affirmed that the Pope was the universal head of the church. The East did not.
    - The Western church taught that the Holy Spirit proceeded from the Father and the Son. The East argued that the Holy Spirit proceeded only from the Father.
    - The Western church came to affirm the doctrine of purgatory, a place of purging after death. The Eastern church did not.
    - The Western church did not allow priests to marry. But the Eastern church would allow priests to be married prior to ordination (bishops could not marry, however).
    - The Western church practiced baptism in different ways including by immersion but also by pouring. The Eastern church practiced threefold immersion.
    - The Western church used unleavened bread in communion. The East used leavened bread.
10. The Eastern branch
11. The Second Council of Nicaea
12. The Filioque Clause
13. Michael Cerularius and Cardinal Humbert
14. Roman Catholicism

15. Exact list will vary. Answers may include:
    - Protestants believe in the supreme authority of Scripture. In Eastern Orthodoxy, Scripture, tradition, and the ecumenical councils are given equal weight in determining faith and practice.
    - Protestants believe in two sacraments or ordinances (Baptism and the Lord's Supper). Eastern Orthodoxy affirms seven sacraments (Baptism, Communion, Chrismation, Confession, Unction, Marriage, and Ordination).
    - Protestants in most cases, receive the addition of the clause "And the Son" in the Nicene Creed. Eastern Orthodoxy does not.
    - Protestants do not use icons or statues in their worship. Eastern Orthodoxy makes extensive use of icons.
    - Protestants believe in salvation by grace, through faith alone for all who trust in Jesus Christ. Eastern Orthodoxy teaches salvation as a process of theosis or deification. We must participate in this process. This does not mean we actually become gods, but we become like God in his divine nature (purified, resurrected, and living eternally with God).
    - Protestants maintain that the Old Testament canon consists of 39 books. Eastern Orthodoxy receives additional books (known as Apocrypha or Deutero-Canonical books) consisting of some 49 books in the Old Testament canon.
16. We are called to walk in lowliness, gentleness, longsuffering, and bearing with one another in love.
17. Divisions have the effect of proving genuine disciples in contrast with counterfeit believers.

UNIT 2 EXAM: THE EARLY MIDDLE AGES

1. e
2. g
3. a
4. i
5. b
6. c
7. j
8. d
9. f
10. h
11. f
12. h
13. d
14. a
15. j
16. b
17. c
18. e
19. g
20. i
21. C
22. B
23. D
24. A
25. B
26. C
27. D
28. B
29. B
30. C
31. D
32. B
33. A
34. B
35. C
36. D
37. A
38. C
39. D
40. A

UNIT 2 ESSAY: THE EARLY MIDDLE AGES

Graded by parent/teacher

UNIT 2 OPTIONAL ENRICHMENT PROJECTS

Graded by parent/teacher

CHAPTER 12: UNIVERSITIES AND SCHOLASTICISM

1. f
2. d
3. e
4. a

5. h
6. c
7. g
8. b
9. University of Bologna
10. Lecture and disputation
11. Often, young people engaged in foolish and ungodly behavior due to the lack of parental discipline and supervision.
12. University of Paris
13. Aristotle
14. *Cur Deus Homo* (Why the God Man?)
15. The distinction between mortal sins and venial sins.
16. Paul warns that knowledge can have the effect of "puffing up" (i.e. making one prideful). He also warns everyone to realize that their knowledge is limited. If someone thinks they know something to the full extent, they do not yet know the matter as they ought to know.
17. Answers will vary. Agur confesses that he is "stupid" or "brutish" and has very little understanding of wisdom and knowledge of the Holy One. Agur is not saying that he knows absolutely nothing. Rather, he is reflecting on just how little he knows in light of God's greatness. It is important that we are humble concerning the things we do not know or understand. Nevertheless, the Bible is a sure foundation for knowledge. Whatever God reveals in His Word is truth.

CHAPTER 13: MONASTICISM IN THE MIDDLE AGES

1. d
2. a
3. f
4. b
5. c
6. e
7. The Fourth Lateran Council. AD 1215.
8. Citeaux
9. Clear valley
10. Bernard supported the Second Crusade to defend the Holy Land against the Muslims.
11. It began with the Fourth Lateran Council in AD 1215 which authorized the destruction of the Cathars.
12. The Rule of St. Augustine
13. Mendicant refers to the practice of begging.
14. Schaff commented that monasticism was the "chief centre of true religion as well as of dark superstition."
15. Answers will vary.

CHAPTER 14: THE PAPAL SCHISM AND THE CONCILIAR MOVEMENT

1. d
2. f
3. a
4. e
5. b
6. c
7. One must be in subjection to the Roman pope in order to be saved.
8. 1347
9. Gregory XI
10. Peter d'Ailly and John Gerson
11. Pope Eugenius IV
12. John Huss
13. Summary will vary. Faithful elders should shepherd God's flock with a willing heart, not seeking to enrich themselves financially, but serving with an eager heart. Elders should not use their authority over the flock in a domineering and unloving way. Instead, they should be examples of godliness to the flock. The popes were first, occupying an unbiblical office. But as bishops or overseers of the wider church, they were also poor examples because many of them sought dishonest gain, they lorded their authority over others for their own selfish pursuits, and they often were very poor examples of godliness.
14. Paul teaches us that faction and team building in the church is fleshly. To claim to be following one church leader against another when the church has one head: Jesus Christ, is fleshly.

ANSWER KEY

CHAPTER 15: REFORM EFFORTS IN THE MIDDLE AGES

1. c
2. a
3. b
4. f
5. d
6. h
7. e
8. g
9. Lyons
10. The Council of Verona. AD 1184
11. Matthew 5:33-34
12. Piedmont
13. A new English translation of the Bible produced from Wycliffe's work and completed by John Purvey. It was an English translation based on the Latin Vulgate translation of the Bible.
14. The Lollards
15. The Bohemian Brethren or the Moravian Brethren
16. Jesus warns against the sinful fear of man. It is important to remember that men can only harm our bodies, but not our souls. But God has the power to cast both body and soul into hell. Examples from this chapter will vary.

UNIT 3 EXAM: THE LATE MIDDLE AGES

1. f
2. h
3. a
4. c
5. b
6. d
7. j
8. e
9. g
10. i
11. g
12. c
13. i
14. a
15. h
16. e
17. b
18. j
19. d
20. f
21. B
22. C
23. B
24. A
25. D
26. B
27. C
28. B
29. A
30. D
31. D
32. A
33. C
34. C
35. B
36. B
37. C
38. A
39. A
40. D

UNIT 3 ESSAY: THE LATE MIDDLE AGES

Graded by parent/teacher

UNIT 3 OPTIONAL ENRICHMENT PROJECTS

Graded by parent/teacher

CHAPTER 16: THE DAWN OF THE REFORMATION

1. f
2. a
3. d
4. b
5. c
6. h
7. e
8. g
9. The invention of the printing press made it much easier for the Protestant Reformers to broadcast their message to the people of Europe.
10. "Back to the sources"

11. Johannes Reuchlin
12. A new Latin translation of the New Testament along with the text of the original Greek New Testament in parallel columns.
13. Julius II

CHAPTER 17: THE REFORMATION IN GERMANY

1. 1505
2. Erfurt
3. 1510
4. 1517
5. Wittenberg
6. Wartburg
7. Worms
8. The Scala Sancta
9. Bible
10. Previous to 1519, Luther thought the phrase "the righteousness of God" in Romans 1 referred to God's righteous judgment upon sinners. Finally, Luther understood what Paul was saying. God's righteousness is revealed in the gospel as the righteousness that God Himself provides for sinners, through His Son Jesus Christ. It was in these words that Luther understood what Paul was teaching about justification by faith.
11. Johann Tetzel
12. Johann Eck
13. Luther translated the New Testament from Greek into German.
14. The Black Cloister in Wittenberg
15. *A Mighty Fortress is Our God*
16. Paul says that the gospel is the power of God unto salvation to all who believe. Answers will vary. To know that the gospel is powerful should give us confidence that when we share it, the Lord is mighty to save, and God can powerfully save sinners through faith in Christ.

CHAPTER 18: THE SWISS REFORMATION IN ZURICH

1. d
2. f
3. g
4. a
5. c
6. b
7. e
8. h
9. Glarus and Einsiedeln
10. Desiderius Erasmus
11. A terrible plague swept through Zurich
12. The reason this sausage meal was so controversial and important is because it violated a long-established church tradition. The meal occurred during the forty-day observance of Lent, which commemorated Jesus' forty-day temptation in the wilderness. Roman church authorities required people to abstain from eating meat during Lent even though the Bible did not require such fasting.
13. Felix Manz
14. The disagreement left unresolved was the difference in perspectives on the presence of Christ in the Lord's Supper. Zwingli and Luther disagreed on this matter.
15. Zwingli died in battle near Kappel seeking to defend Zurich from the Catholic cantons.
16. Paul commands Timothy to preach the Word of God. Answers will vary depending on Bible translation consulted. The NKJV uses the words "convince, rebuke, and exhort" to describe different aspects of preaching God's Word.
17. Zwingli and other reformers in Zurich believed that all imagery and statues ought to be removed from the churches to purify God's worship. Applications made by the student will vary.

CHAPTER 19: THE ANABAPTIST MOVEMENT

1. d
2. a
3. f
4. b
5. c
6. e
7. The Lutheran stream, the Reformed stream, and the Anabaptist stream
8. Zurich
9. Pouring (also known as "effusion")
10. Ulrich Zwingli
11. The *Schleitheim Confession*

12. Melchior Hoffman
13. Menno Simons
14. Answers will vary.
15. Answers will vary. Any prophet who proclaims false religion or worship (idolatry) was to be put to death in Old Testament Israel. But if one was to ascertain whether the prophet was a true prophet, one could look at their prophecies and whether the word they said came to pass.

CHAPTER 20: THE REFORMATION IN GENEVA
1. d
2. f
3. b
4. g
5. a
6. c
7. h
8. e
9. Nicolas Cop
10. 1538
11. St. Pierre's Cathedral
12. The Trinity, the deity of Christ, and original sin
13. Brazil
14. Paul refers to preaching all of the essential truths of God's Word to the Ephesians. There was no doctrine that Paul left out in his presentation of the Word of God. Answers will vary. Pastors should be committed to preaching all of God's Word knowing that the entire Bible was given for the benefit of Christ's disciples. Pastors should not hold anything back in their preaching if it is found in God's Word.
15. The seven men appointed to serve as deacons in the church relieved the burden of caring for the widow's needs in the daily distribution of food. This enabled the apostles to focus on the ministry of the word and prayer, but also meant that the practical service of food distribution was not neglected either.

CHAPTER 21: WILLIAM TYNDALE AND THE ENGLISH BIBLE
1. d
2. a
3. f
4. b
5. c
6. e
7. Around 85% to 90%
8. Cuthbert Tunstall
9. Worms
10. This scheme had the effect of funding Tyndale's second edition of the English New Testament.
11. Henry Phillips
12. "Lord, open the king of England's eyes"
13. The Word of God is to be treasured above gold and silver. It is far more valuable than any earthly riches.
14. The Word of God is like a hammer that breaks rocks in pieces. Answers will vary.

CHAPTER 22: THE REFORMATION IN ENGLAND
1. 1533
2. 1549
3. 1553
4. 1556
5. 1558, 1603
6. Oxford
7. Catherine had not given Henry VIII a surviving male heir.
8. Anne Boleyn
9. An annulment is a declaration by the church that a marriage was not valid to begin with, and therefore the relationship can be dissolved.
10. Thomas Cranmer
11. "Bloody Mary"
12. It brought a period of stability to the Church of England through the Elizabethan settlement. The church was established as a Protestant church with Reformed doctrine. But it retained some Roman Catholic elements in its worship and church government.
13. Peter calls the Word a light shining in a dark place.
14. King Josiah is described as walking in all of the Lord's ways, and not turning aside to the right or to the left (meaning he stayed on the Lord's path and did not turn to his own ways). Edward VI was

a godly king like Josiah. He sought to obey the Word of God, and to reign as King in accord with God's instructions.

CHAPTER 23: THE REFORMATION IN SCOTLAND

1. d
2. g
3. b
4. a
5. c
6. h
7. e
8. f
9. John Knox
10. George Wishart
11. The Castle at St. Andrews
12. Berwick-on-Tweed
13. Knox stated: "The most perfect school of Christ that ever was in the earth since the days of the apostles. In other places I confess Christ to be truly preached; but manners and religion so sincerely reformed, I have not yet seen in any other place."
14. The *Scottish Confession* of 1560.
15. Paul likens the work of ministry to being a soldier. Those engaged in warfare as a soldier must expect to endure hardship and difficulty. The soldier does not follow his own desires, but instead submits to the orders of his commanding officer. Answers will vary. Knox suffered hardship in serving the Lord Jesus Christ, and always sought to be faithful to the Word of Christ.
16. Knox was similar to the prophet Micaiah in his interviews with Queen Mary by faithfully speaking God's Word, even when it was considered offensive.

CHAPTER 24: THE CATHOLIC COUNTER REFORMATION

1. e
2. a
3. g
4. b
5. c
6. h
7. d
8. f
9. Martin Bucer, Philip Melanchthon, John Calvin
10. Ignatius Loyola
11. Francis Xavier
12. The Council of Trent
13. Aristotle and Thomas Aquinas
14. King Louis XIV
15. Paul warns that anyone who preaches a different gospel is accursed, or damned to eternal hell. The Roman Catholics used the same language of "accursed" (anathema) in denouncing the Protestants. By doing so, the Roman Catholic Church proclaimed accursed those who actually held to the true gospel.

UNIT 4 EXAM: THE REFORMATION

1. d
2. f
3. h
4. b
5. a
6. c
7. i
8. j
9. g
10. e
11. d
12. a
13. g
14. b
15. i
16. c
17. e
18. j
19. f
20. h
21. B
22. D
23. C
24. D
25. A
26. C
27. B

ANSWER KEY

28. B
29. A
30. C
31. B
32. A
33. B
34. C
35. A
36. D
37. B
38. C
39. B
40. A

UNIT 4 ESSAY (THE REFORMATION)

Graded by parent/teacher

UNIT 4 OPTIONAL ENRICHMENT PROJECTS

Graded by parent/teacher

CHAPTER 25: PURITANS, SEPARATISTS, AND COVENANTERS

1. d
2. f
3. a
4. h
5. b
6. c
7. e
8. g
9. Episcopal, Presbyterian, and Congregational
10. Separatists
11. The Hampton Court Conference
12. Jenny Geddes
13. The Westminster Assembly
14. The Great Fire of London
15. The Lord Jesus Christ's goal is to sanctify and cleanse his bride, the church, from all sin. One day, the church will be completely perfected, and cleansed of all impurities.
16. God promises to dwell with us and walk among us. We will be His people and He will be our God. The command is to cleanse ourselves from all idolatry and impurity to be God's holy people who are set apart from the ways of this world.

CHAPTER 26: PIETISTS, ARMINIANS, AND BAPTISTS

1. e
2. c
3. a
4. b
5. h
6. d
7. f
8. g
9. Gustavus Adolphus
10. *The Book of Concord*
11. Philip Jakob Spener
12. A small-group gathering of Christians for Bible study, prayer, and mutual edification.
13. "On the watch for the Lord"
14. Jacob Arminius
15. Charles Spurgeon
16. We are to spur one another on to love and good works. Answers will vary. We are to assemble together in worship and fellowship to exhort one another toward faith and love.

CHAPTER 27: CHRISTIANITY IN COLONIAL AMERICA

1. c
2. a
3. f
4. h
5. b
6. d
7. e
8. g
9. Jamestown
10. The *Mayflower*
11. A: In Adam's fall, we sinned all.
12. The colony of Maryland allowed Roman Catholics freedom of worship.
13. Pennsylvania
14. False hopes listed in these verses include large armies, human strength, and horses. Our solid hope is the Lord who can deliver us. Answers will vary.

CHAPTER 28: THE GREAT AWAKENING

1. d
2. a
3. b
4. c
5. d
6. a
7. b
8. e
9. c
10. 6,500 hymns
11. John Newton and William Cowper
12. The student may summarize Packer's quote in their own words. Packer stated: "The visitation of God which brings to life Christians who have been sleeping and restores a deep sense of God's near presence and holiness. Thence springs a vivid sense of sin and a profound exercise of heart in repentance, praise, and love, with an evangelistic outflow."
13. When God revives His people, they rejoice in Him. The effect of God giving spiritual life is joy in God.

CHAPTER 29: APOSTASY AND DOCTRINAL DECLINE IN THE CHURCH

1. d
2. c
3. h
4. a
5. g
6. b
7. e
8. f
9. Unitarians deny the doctrine of the Trinity and believe that God is only one person.
10. Deism is the belief that there is a God who exists. But this God has no interaction with human creatures. He is like a watchmaker. He created the world like a man makes a watch, then wound it up and left it to run its own course according to natural laws. Deists denied miracles, the supernatural, and God's providential hand in history. The Deists affirmed the existence of some god. But they rejected the Bible as God's revelation of Himself.
11. Julius Wellhausen (1844-1918) developed the Documentary Hypothesis in the 1870s. In this "hypothesis," Wellhausen claimed that Moses was not the author of the first five books of the Bible. Instead, Wellhausen identified four different unnamed authors. These four authors combined and then added material. The eventual result was the first five books of the Bible (the Pentateuch).
12. This passage states that every Word God has spoken is pure. The Word of God is without flaws. If we add our own ideas to God's Word, we will be rebuked by the Lord and found to be liars.

UNIT 5 EXAM: THE POST-REFORMATION PERIOD

1. f
2. i
3. a
4. b
5. c
6. d
7. e
8. g
9. j
10. h
11. e
12. c
13. a
14. g
15. d
16. b
17. i
18. f
19. j
20. h
21. A
22. C
23. D
24. B
25. C
26. B
27. D
28. A

ANSWER KEY 165

29. B
30. C
31. A
32. D
33. A
34. A
35. B
36. C
37. D
38. C
39. C
40. D

UNIT 5 ESSAY: THE POST-REFORMATION
Graded by parent/teacher

UNIT 5 OPTIONAL ENRICHMENT PROJECTS
Graded by parent/teacher

CHAPTER 30: THE MODERN MISSIONARY MOVEMENT
1. c
2. f
3. a
4. g
5. b
6. h
7. d
8. e
9. The 19th century
10. Six years
11. The burning of widows on the funeral pyre of their husbands.
12. The Anglo-Burmese War
13. Tanna
14. The promise of this passage is that all the nations of the earth will turn and remember the Lord and worship him. This should give us confidence that the mission of Jesus Christ will be ultimately successful.

CHAPTER 31: REVIVALS AND CULTS IN THE 19TH CENTURY
1. d
2. a
3. f
4. b
5. c
6. g
7. h
8. e
9. Asahel Nettleton
10. Charles Grandison Finney
11. Barton Stone and Alexander Campbell
12. Charles Taze Russell
13. The Church of Jesus Christ of Latter Day Saints (LDS), or Mormons
14. Llangeitho
15. This passage warns us that not every "spirit" (i.e. teacher or movement) is from God. It warns us that there are many false prophets and we should be on guard against them.
16. Jesus promises that if we ask for the Holy Spirit, God the Father will give it those who ask Him.

CHAPTER 32: FUNDAMENTALISTS AND LIBERALS
1. g
2. c
3. a
4. b
5. d
6. h
7. e
8. f
9. "A God without wrath brought men without sin into a kingdom without judgment through the ministrations of a Christ without a cross."
10. *The Fundamentals*
11. Westminster Theological Seminary
12. The Orthodox Presbyterian Church
13. The death and resurrection of Jesus Christ in accord with the prophecies of the Scriptures.
14. If the resurrection of Christ did not actually happen, then our faith in Christ is vain, and we are false witnesses if we proclaim the resurrection.

CHAPTER 33: PERSECUTIONS IN EASTERN EUROPE
1. c

2. f
3. a
4. b
5. g
6. d
7. e
8. h
9. The Russian Orthodox Church
10. Joseph Stalin
11. Brother Andrew often prayed that the eyes of border guards would be closed so that he could smuggle Bibles into Eastern Europe.
12. Romania
13. In 1917, the estimate was 1,800 churches. By 1921, the number had dropped to 160.
14. The saints are those who keep God's commandments, and the faith of (or "in") Jesus. If we want to know who a Christian is, we can see if someone keeps God's commandments and if they believe in the Lord Jesus Christ.
15. Like the three men of Daniel 3, Richard Wurmbrand opposed the idolatry of the communists by refusing to bow down to the communist leaders who opposed the one true God.

CHAPTER 34: CHRISTIANS IN WORLD WAR II

1. c
2. a
3. e
4. b
5. f
6. d
7. h
8. g
9. Germany invaded Poland, setting off conflict in Europe.
10. 60 million people
11. *The Hiding Place*
12. Nuremberg, Germany
13. Herman Goering
14. Answers will vary.

CHAPTER 35: PERSECUTIONS IN CHINA AND KOREA

1. China
2. 1980
3. 1907
4. 1950, 1953
5. 1900
6. Shansi District
7. Mao Zedong
8. Brother Yun
9. Jonathan Goforth and William Blair
10. Answers will vary. This passage helps us to remember that we are not at war with people. Our battle is not with flesh and blood. Instead, we are at war with the spiritual forces of darkness which oppose Jesus Christ. We need the armor of God to stand against these forces.

CHAPTER 36: CHRISTIAN LEADERS AND MOVEMENTS OF THE 20TH CENTURY

1. c
2. a
3. e
4. b
5. f
6. d
7. h
8. g
9. He was a medical doctor.
10. Answers will vary. She returned to minister to the Waorani tribe who had killed her husband.
11. In Los Angeles, during the Azusa Street Revival
12. John Dewey
13. Young-Earth Creationism
14. The Global South
15. One day, every person in the world will bow the knee to Jesus Christ and confess Him to be Lord over all.

UNIT 6 EXAM: THE AGE OF MISSIONS AND THE MODERN PERIOD

1. j
2. a
3. e
4. h
5. b
6. c

7. d
8. f
9. g
10. i
11. b
12. g
13. c
14. f
15. a
16. d
17. j
18. e
19. i
20. h
21. B
22. D
23. C
24. D
25. A
26. C
27. B
28. A
29. D
30. B
31. A
32. C
33. B
34. D
35. A
36. C
37. B
38. C
39. A
40. B

UNIT 6 ESSAY: THE AGE OF MISSIONS AND THE MODERN PERIOD

Graded by parent/teacher

UNIT 6 OPTIONAL ENRICHMENT PROJECTS

Graded by parent/teacher